ORCHESTRAL INSTRUMENTS

M

THE SCRIBNER GUIDE TO

ORCHESTRAL INSTRUMENTS

The Diagram Group

CHARLES SCRIBNER'S SONS, NEW YORK

Library of Congress Cataloging in Publication Data
Main entry under title:

The Scribner guide to orchestral instruments.

Previously published as part of: Musical
Instruments of the World. 1976.
Includes index.
1.Musical instruments. 2.Orchestra. I.Diagram
Group. II.Title.
ML460.07 1983   781.91   83.3239
ISBN 0-684-179512

1 3 5 7 9 11 13 15 17 19 Q/C 20 18 16 12 10 8 6 4 2

Printed in the United States of America.

Contents

Foreword

The symphony orchestra is now so much a part of the modern musical scene that it is easy for the music lover and concert goer to take it for granted. The widespread availability of recorded music in recent years has made this especially true. But what lies behind the modern orchestra? How is it made up? How has it developed over the centuries? Why has it evolved in a particular way? And most important, what of the instruments themselves? What have been the major factors in their development?

This book attempts to answer some of these questions by highlighting each instrument in turn and demonstrating its role and importance in the orchestra. First, however, a brief account of the symphony orchestra and a summary of its evolution will serve as a background.

The modern symphony orchestra
The instruments which comprise the standard symphony orchestra are: flutes, oboes, clarinets, bassoons, horns, trumpets, trombones, timpani, first and second violins, violas, violoncellos, and double basses. Extra instruments such as piccolo, cor anglais or English horn, different sizes of clarinet, contrabassoon, tuba, harp, drums, and percussion may also be required in some larger works. The strings form the backbone of the orchestra, playing almost throughout a composition, with the more distinctive tone colors of the woodwinds and brass reserved for solo and special effect passages, and, of course, the loud *tutti* sections in which all the instruments play together.

Development
In the history of music, the orchestra is a comparatively recent phenomenon. Its evolution began in the late 16th century when composers started to turn their attention from writing vocal part-music, or polyphony, to composing specifically for instrumental groups. Composers such as Monteverdi around 1600 began to recognize the individual tone colors of different instruments and put them to good effect,

especially in dramatic works. These were not the orchestral instruments that we know today, but the lutes, cornetts, and high trumpets which gave the instrumental music of the Renaissance its characteristic flavor. Nevertheless, the seeds of the modern orchestra had been planted and were to grow over the centuries, finally blossoming in the 1800s.

During the 17th century composers began to favor bowed stringed instruments since their sound tended to be sweeter, more expressive and easier to control than the wind instruments of the time. So developed the string group which was to become the heart of the symphony orchestra. A well known example of such an orchestra is Lully's "Vingt-quatre violons du Roi" at the French court of the late 17th century. Though other instruments were occasionally added to this basic group, one instrument always present in a baroque orchestra was the harpsichord. Not only was it used to amplify and fill out the rather thin string harmonies, but its player directed all performances from the keyboard, fulfilling the same function as the conductor a century or more later.

Inseparably connected with the development of the orchestra are improvements in the construction of musical instruments, progress in the art of composition, and developments in the technique of performance. The technical limitations of instruments, particularly the woodwinds and brass, have meant that they were not accepted as regular members of the orchestra until many years after they first appeared. In fact, the problems of reducing an instrument's technical limitations have taxed instrument makers for centuries.

By the early 18th century, the period of J. S. Bach and Handel, improvements had been made to some instruments, progress had been made in the technique of performance, and certain effective instrumental combinations had been formulated. Flutes, oboes of different sizes, horns, and trumpets were the instruments most commonly found in partnership with the strings in a typical orchestra of the 18th century. While its basic make up remained unchanged throughout the century, changes were made in composers' treatment of the instruments. Rameau (1683–1764) was one of the first composers to give really interesting melodic passages to the flutes, oboes, and bassoons, thus preparing the way for the coloristic treatment of instruments in the modern orchestra.

By the time of Mozart and Haydn, most European courts and opera houses had their own orchestras. A typical classical orchestra would have pairs of flutes, oboes, clarinets, bassoons, horns, trumpets, and timpani; violins in two parts, violas, violoncellos and double basses. It is interesting to note that the clarinet was the last of the woodwind to be adopted as a regular member of the orchestra since it was an instrument which was actually invented rather than one which had evolved over a century or more.

During the 19th century composers such as Berlioz, Liszt, Wagner, and Richard Strauss began to focus on the particular tone colors of individual instruments and produced very imaginatively scored orchestral works. A number of new instruments was developed at this time to fulfil composers' requirements for a greater variety of tone color. This century also

Below Usual orchestral seating plan. Instruments of the four "families" — woodwind, brass, percussion, and strings — are positioned in groups. This arrangement helps blend the tone colors of individual instruments, and helps the musicians play together in their groups.

Woodwind	Brass
1 Piccolo	9 Horns
2 Flutes	10 Trumpets
3 Oboes	11 Trombones
4 Cor anglais	12 Tuba
5 Clarinets	
6 Bass clarinet	
7 Bassoons	
8 Contrabassoon	

Percussion	Strings
13 Tam-tam	21 Harp
14 Cymbals	22 1st violins
15 Xylophone	23 2nd violins
16 Glockenspiel	24 Violas
17 Tubular bells	25 Cellos
18 Side drum	26 Double basses
19 Bass drum	
20 Timpani	

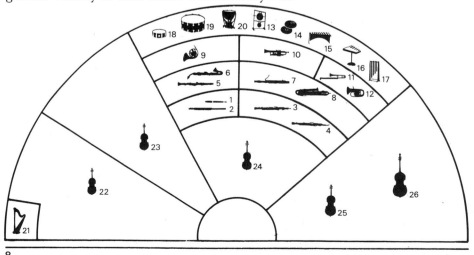

saw an interest in improving existing instruments, and great strides were made especially in the field of woodwind keywork and brass valve systems, giving instruments greater reliability, better intonation, and improved melodic flexibility.

With more and more instruments available to them, composers began to take advantage of this and write for larger and larger resources. This tendency is well illustrated by some of the scores of Mahler (1860–1911). His Eighth Symphony, for example, is scored for piccolo, four flutes, four oboes, English horn, E♭ clarinet, three B♭ clarinets, bass clarinet, four bassoons, contrabassoon, eight horns, four trumpets, four trombones, tuba, timpani, bass drum, cymbals, tam-tam, triangle, chimes, glockenspiel, celesta, piano, harmonium, organ, two harps, mandolin, four fanfare trumpets and three fanfare trombones, seven vocal soloists, two mixed choruses, boys' choir, first and second violins, violas, violoncellos, and double basses.

Below The comparative pitch ranges of common orchestral instruments, shown in relation to the piano keyboard. In the case of instruments — like the clarinet and trumpet — for which written notation differs from actual sound, the diagram gives the actual sound produced.

©DIAGRAM

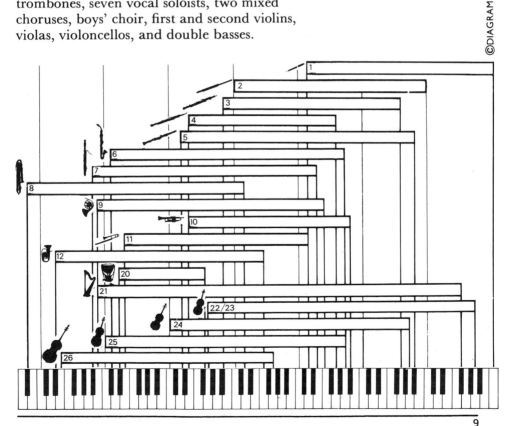

After the comparative excesses of the late 19th century and early 1900s, more recent composers have been inclined to use instruments more sparingly for both artistic and economic reasons! Contemporary composers have, in many cases, returned to scoring their works on the basis of musical requirements rather than on the availability of the "standard" symphony orchestra. But, of course, the orchestra continues to thrive since the greater part of its repertoire—and the part which audiences are most keen to hear—is drawn from the orchestral works of the 18th and 19th centuries. In addition, the orchestra is an almost perfect medium for musical expression; like an artist's palette, it has a multitude of different colors just waiting to be mixed with skill and flair to provide exactly the right shade and texture.

Using this book
The basic classification of instruments within this book is derived from the system published in 1914 by Erich von Hornbostel and Curt Sachs. Under this system instruments are classified according to the way in which the sound is produced. Orchestral instruments fall into four of these main groups—aerophones or woodwind and brass, membranophones or drums, idiophones or percussion, and chordophones or strings. Each of the chapters is devoted to instruments of a particular category, and within each chapter instruments are arranged in the order in which they appear in a musical score—generally from highest to lowest. Every chapter explains the nature of a single group of instruments, providing technical accounts and simple accompanying diagrams to illustrate the

Below Alternative seating plans for an orchestra. The commonest plan (a) has flutes, oboes, clarinets, and bassoons in a block at the center of the orchestra. Some conductors, however, prefer these players in a single line (b), while others favor the separation of first and second violins (c).

Woodwind	Brass
1 Piccolo	9 Horns
2 Flutes	10 Trumpets
3 Oboes	11 Trombones
4 Cor anglais	12 Tuba
5 Clarinets	
6 Bass clarinet	
7 Bassoons	
8 Contrabassoon	

Percussion	Strings
13 Tam-tam	21 Harp
14 Cymbals	22 1st violins
15 Xylophone	23 2nd violins
16 Glockenspiel	24 Violas
17 Tubular bells	25 Cellos
18 Side drum	26 Double basses
19 Bass drum	
20 Timpani	

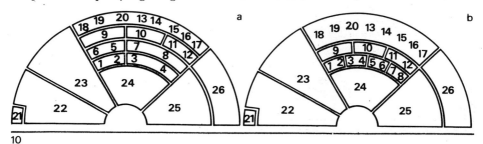

characteristics of the instruments forming that group. Furthermore, the chapter introductions demonstrate exactly how familiar orchestral instruments fit into the overall picture of instruments throughout the world, from the simplest to the most complex.

Each instrument is described in detail and there is a reference panel which contains a section of score for that instrument, a list of compositions featuring that instrument, a figure demonstrating the correct playing position, and a diagram indicating its customary location in the orchestra. For the sake of completeness, instruments not normally part of the orchestra but sometimes used as soloists in concertos have also been included. Among these are the guitar and the piano.

This is not only a coherent exposé of the modern orchestra but also a book to dip into. Each chapter is complete in itself but is at the same time an interlocking piece in the complete jigsaw of sounds that make up the modern symphony orchestra.

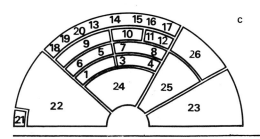

c

1

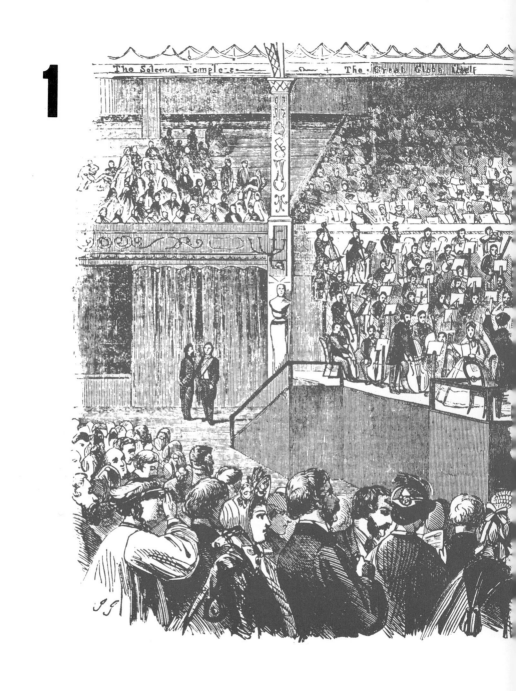

Aerophones: introduction

Aerophones are instruments in which the sound is produced by the vibration of air. They are classified according to how the vibration is generated, and include flutes, reeds, cup mouthpiece instruments, and free aerophones. Since the Stone Age, flutes have been endowed with magical significance, and some peoples still use them in ritual associated with storms, crops, and death. Reed instruments originated in the East. More complex than flutes, they are less widely distributed, appearing today in Europe, Africa, and the East. Cup mouthpiece instruments have a very ancient history. Found in varying degrees of sophistication throughout the world, they are today most commonly used for ritual, military, and signaling purposes. Free aerophones, typified by the bull-roarer, are still used by some tribes as magical instruments.

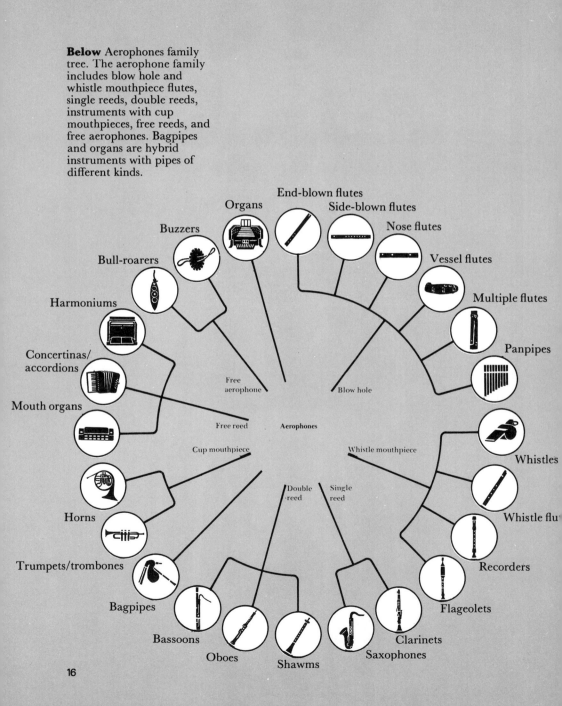

Below Aerophones family tree. The aerophone family includes blow hole and whistle mouthpiece flutes, single reeds, double reeds, instruments with cup mouthpieces, free reeds, and free aerophones. Bagpipes and organs are hybrid instruments with pipes of different kinds.

End-blown flutes

Organs

Side-blown flutes

Nose flutes

Buzzers

Vessel flutes

Bull-roarers

Multiple flutes

Harmoniums

Panpipes

Concertinas/ accordions

Mouth organs

Free aerophone

Blow hole

Free reed

Aerophones

Whistles

Cup mouthpiece

Whistle mouthpiece

Horns

Double reed

Single reed

Whistle flu

Trumpets/trombones

Recorders

Bagpipes

Flageolets

Bassoons

Oboes

Shawms

Clarinets

Saxophones

Below Making the air vibrate. In all types of aerophone sound is made by vibrating air, and instruments are classified according to how the air is set into vibration. In instruments with a blow hole (a) or whistle mouthpiece (b) the air vibrates after being directed against a sharp edge.

Vibrations in a tube may also be produced by reeds—single (c), double (d), or free (e). In cup mouthpiece instruments (f) air is made to vibrate by the action of the player's lips. In a free aerophone (g) there is no enclosed air column—the air vibrates around the instrument as it travels through the air.

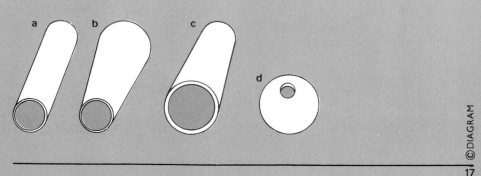

Below Body shapes. Most aerophones have a tubular or vessel-shaped body in which vibrating air is enclosed during play. The shape of the body affects the character of the sound produced. The most common body type is the tube, which may be cylindrical (a) as in the

clarinet, tapering (b) as in the recorder, or flared (c) as in the oboe. Less common are aerophones with a vessel body (d) like that of the ocarina.

Below Pitch. The pitch produced depends on the length of the tube containing the vibrating air column. The tube's length determines the length of the sound waves (frequencies) produced in a second. Any tube is theoretically capable of producing a pitch appropriate to its length. This pitch is called the fundamental. A 2ft tube will sound middle C (1), while a tube twice as long will sound one octave lower (2). A stopped (closed) pipe will sound one octave lower than an unstopped pipe of the same length.

1

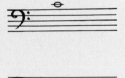 

2

Below Harmonic series. When a column of air is activated it vibrates not only as a whole but in sections. These secondary vibrations produce pitches other than the fundamental. Known as harmonics, these additional pitches are produced by increasing the intensity of the airstream so that the air vibrates more quickly in the tube. Harmonics occur in a sequence called the harmonic series. Although the distance between one harmonic and the next is fixed, the actual pitches vary with the size and shape of the tube. The example given here is for a hypothetical 8ft tube.

1   2   3   4   5   6   7   8   9 10 11 12 13 14 15 16

[Fundamental]

Below Altering the pitch. Only by shortening or lengthening the tube can an aerophone be made to produce pitches other than its fundamental and associated harmonics. A tube is "shortened" by the use of finger holes: opening holes at the lower end of the tube has the effect of reducing the total length of the tube to the point at which air can first escape (a). A longer tube may be obtained by means of a simple slide mechanism (b), or by the use of crooks or valves to divert the air through an extra length of tubing (c).

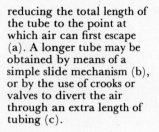

Below Tone color. Every aerophone has its own distinctive sound quality or tone color. When any pitch is played the actual sound produced is colored by the presence of harmonics associated with this pitch. The presence of different harmonics is determined by the shape of the tube. For example, the conical tube of the oboe emphasizes the lower harmonics (a) while the cylindrical tube of the clarinet emphasizes the odd-numbered harmonics (b). (In each case the harmonic composition of the instrument's lowest pitch has been illustrated.)

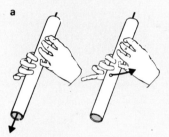

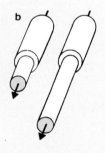

Flutes

The Western classical flute is a side-blown, or transverse, flute that first reached Europe from the East in the 12th century. During the Middle Ages it was chiefly associated with military music, but by the middle of the 17th century had become more important as an instrument of the opera and court orchestra. The first major changes in Western flute design were made in the late 17th century by the French Hotteterre family. Even more important were the radical developments introduced by Theobald Boehm of Munich in the early 1830s. His design has remained largely unaltered until the present day, and "Boehm flutes," made of wood or metal, are today played in symphony orchestras all over the world.

Below The development of keywork on the orchestral flute. The earliest flutes had no keys and some notes were poor in quality and inaccurate in pitch. The addition of keys to correct these defects was a gradual process over 150 years—the earliest keys being added at the instrument's lower end.

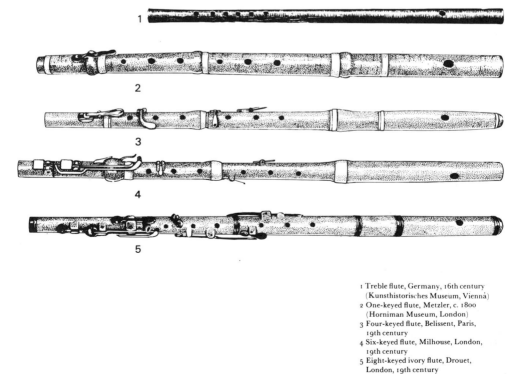

1 Treble flute, Germany, 16th century
  (Kunsthistorisches Museum, Vienna)
2 One-keyed flute, Metzler, c. 1800
  (Horniman Museum, London)
3 Four-keyed flute, Belissent, Paris,
  19th century
4 Six-keyed flute, Milhouse, London,
  19th century
5 Eight-keyed ivory flute, Drouet,
  London, 19th century

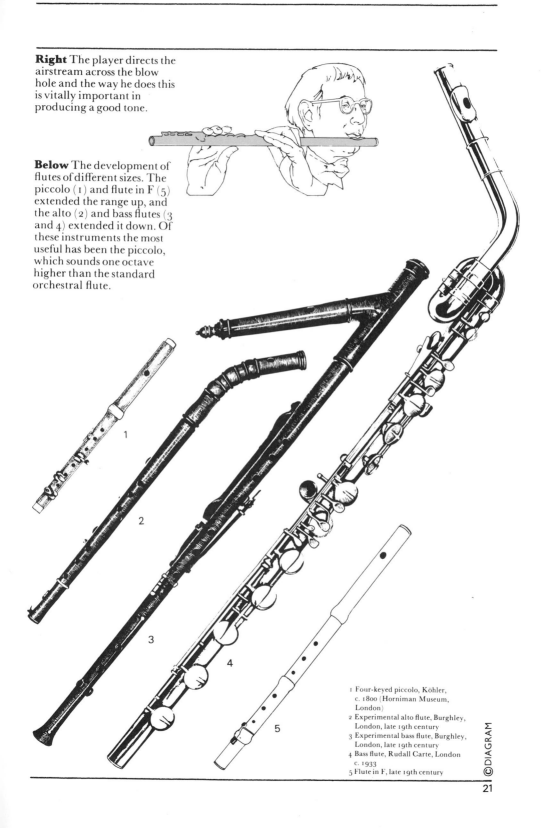

Right The player directs the airstream across the blow hole and the way he does this is vitally important in producing a good tone.

Below The development of flutes of different sizes. The piccolo (1) and flute in F (5) extended the range up, and the alto (2) and bass flutes (3 and 4) extended it down. Of these instruments the most useful has been the piccolo, which sounds one octave higher than the standard orchestral flute.

1

2

3

4

5

1 Four-keyed piccolo, Köhler, c. 1800 (Horniman Museum, London)
2 Experimental alto flute, Burghley, London, late 19th century
3 Experimental bass flute, Burghley, London, late 19th century
4 Bass flute, Rudall Carte, London c. 1933
5 Flute in F, late 19th century

©DIAGRAM

Wiewol Minerve gar miß fälle
Die Pfeif/weil sie den mund verstelt:
Soll man sich doch nicht dr gern loln/
Dann sie red wie ein Weib dar von:

Vnd vil mehr auf Poeten geben
Die solche Pfeif gar hoch erheben/
Weil sie inn der Natur bestehet
Vnd auch zu allen Spilen gehet.

Die Zwerchpfeif erstlich Midas macht
Nur auß Kran:bbeinen vngeschlacht:
Die man darnach macht auß den Roren
Heut kan man sie zum schönsten boren.

5

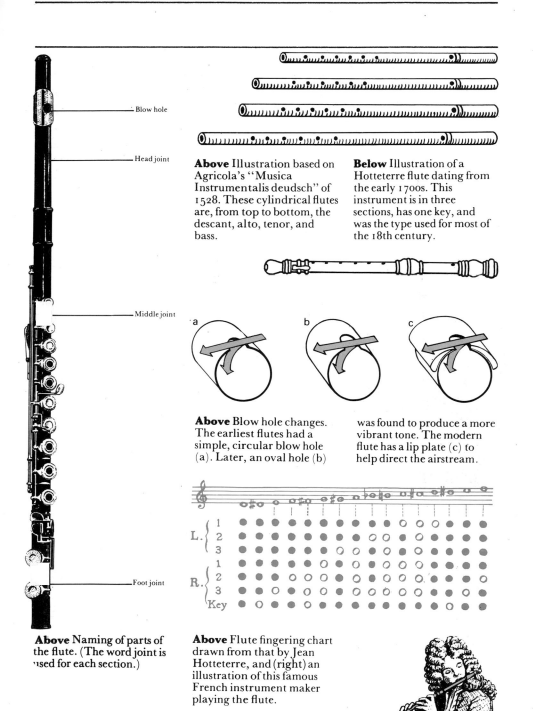

Above Illustration based on Agricola's "Musica Instrumentalis deudsch" of 1528. These cylindrical flutes are, from top to bottom, the descant, alto, tenor, and bass.

Below Illustration of a Hotteterre flute dating from the early 1700s. This instrument is in three sections, has one key, and was the type used for most of the 18th century.

— Blow hole

— Head joint

— Middle joint

— Foot joint

Above Blow hole changes. The earliest flutes had a simple, circular blow hole (a). Later, an oval hole (b) was found to produce a more vibrant tone. The modern flute has a lip plate (c) to help direct the airstream.

Above Naming of parts of the flute. (The word joint is used for each section.)

Above Flute fingering chart drawn from that by Jean Hotteterre, and (right) an illustration of this famous French instrument maker playing the flute.

©DIAGRAM

Below Two Giorgi flutes dating from around 1900. Giorgi was an imaginative Italian instrument maker who sought to develop an alternative to the Boehm flute. These flutes were made of ebonite and were end-blown. Some of his models were without keys whereas others had an unusually large number.

Right Members of the orchestral flute family. The standard flute (1) is prominent in the instrumental texture of chamber and orchestral music, and is also a favorite solo instrument. The piccolo (2) is occasionally used for orchestral solos and for doubling a flute or violin melody an octave higher. As the lower notes of the bass flute (3) and alto flute (4) do not carry well through the orchestral texture, these instruments are usually used in quieter passages where their mellow sound can best be heard.

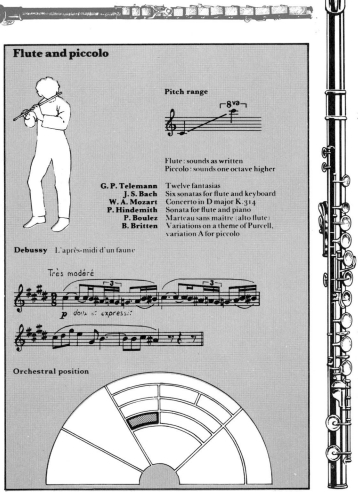

Flute and piccolo

Pitch range

┌─8va─┐

Flute: sounds as written
Piccolo: sounds one octave higher

G. P. Telemann	Twelve fantasias
J. S. Bach	Six sonatas for flute and keyboard
W. A. Mozart	Concerto in D major K.314
P. Hindemith	Sonata for flute and piano
P. Boulez	Marteau sans maître (alto flute)
B. Britten	Variations on a theme of Purcell, variation A for piccolo

Debussy L'après-midi d'un faune

Très modéré

p doux et expressif

Orchestral position

1   3   4

2

Oboes

The oboe was developed from the treble shawm in the 17th century to meet the demand for a shawm-like instrument suitable for indoor use. The first oboes are thought to have been made by the Hotteterre family and were used by musicians at the court of Louis XIV. They were made in three sections, and had accurately calculated bore dimensions and finger hole positions. During the 18th century several different sizes of oboe were introduced into the orchestra. Among them was an alto version—the cor-anglais—which remains in regular use today. The main development in the 19th century was the application of key mechanisms to the oboe. German makers generally preferred a fairly simple mechanism, whereas French makers produced a variety of more complicated systems. Even today, key systems for the oboe vary considerably from maker to maker.

Below The modern reed (a) and the 18th century reed (b) both have a U-shaped scrape and are mounted on a metal staple. The modern staple is covered in cork for a firmer fit in the top of the oboe. The 19th century French reed (c) illustrates a less usual V-shaped scrape.

Right Early oboes. The two-keyed oboe (1) dates from the 17th century and closely resembles the Hotteterre model used in the operas of Lully. The six-keyed oboe of about 1820 (2) has the bulging upper end characteristic of earlier oboes. Its bulbous bell is more typical of larger oboes. The Triébert-system oboe of about 1850 (3), named after its designer, has the smooth elegant profile of the modern instrument.

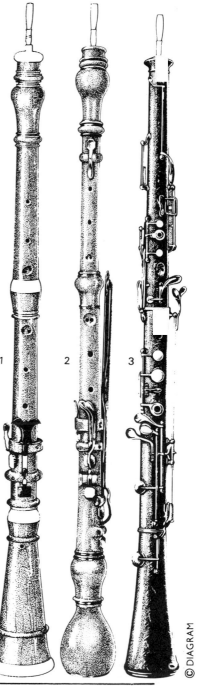

1   2   3

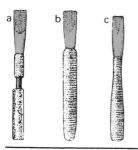

a   b   c

© DIAGRAM

Left Illustrations of modern orchestral oboes and a diagram showing their relative sizes and pitch ranges. The cor anglais (1) is particularly effective when playing melancholy solos. The oboe d'amore (2) was revived in the 19th century for performances of music by J. S. Bach. It has also been used occasionally by 20th century composers. The regular orchestral oboe (3) has been a favorite instrument with composers for almost 300 years. Its reedy sound is heard best either in plaintive melodies or in quick staccato passages.

Right The oboist draws his lips between the teeth into the mouth, and then forces air through the reed at high pressure. Only a little air can be exhaled through such a small opening, and before inhaling again the player must take care to expel unused air from the lungs.

Left Modern baritone oboe (1) and heckelphone (2). The baritone oboe is pitched one octave below the regular orchestral oboe. It is only rarely used. The heckelphone was invented by Heckel in 1904 and has a wide conical bore and bulbous bell. It is usually pitched at baritone range.

1
2

Oboe, oboe d'amore, and cor anglais

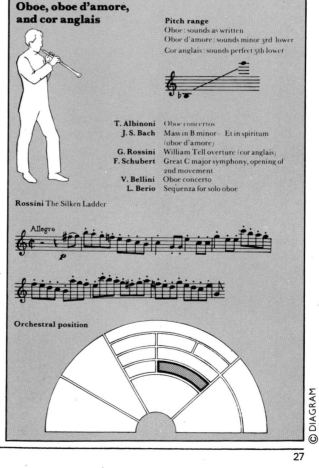

Pitch range
Oboe: sounds as written
Oboe d'amore: sounds minor 3rd lower
Cor anglais: sounds perfect 5th lower

T. Albinoni	Oboe concertos
J. S. Bach	Mass in B minor – Et in spiritum (oboe d'amore)
G. Rossini	William Tell overture (cor anglais)
F. Schubert	Great C major symphony, opening of 2nd movement
V. Bellini	Oboe concerto
L. Berio	Sequenza for solo oboe

Rossini The Silken Ladder

Allegro

Orchestral position

© DIAGRAM

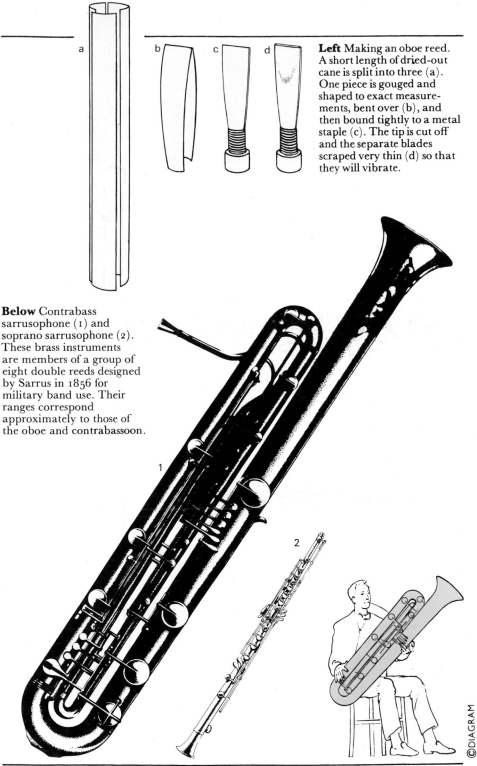

Left Making an oboe reed. A short length of dried-out cane is split into three (a). One piece is gouged and shaped to exact measurements, bent over (b), and then bound tightly to a metal staple (c). The tip is cut off and the separate blades scraped very thin (d) so that they will vibrate.

Below Contrabass sarrusophone (1) and soprano sarrusophone (2). These brass instruments are members of a group of eight double reeds designed by Sarrus in 1856 for military band use. Their ranges correspond approximately to those of the oboe and contrabassoon.

©DIAGRAM

Clarinets

The orchestral clarinet is one of the most versatile of all orchestral instruments. It was first developed from the chalumeau around 1700 by the German instrument-maker J. C. Denner. Over a period of about 20 years the clarinet became distinguishable from the chalumeau by its separate mouthpiece, its bell, and the addition of extra keys which enabled it to play higher notes. In the 1840s the Boehm system of keys, already successfully applied to the orchestral flute, was added to the clarinet. It brought a new facility to clarinet playing and remains the favored system for modern instruments. Throughout its history the clarinet has been made in different sizes. There are also a number of related single-reed instruments, of which the basset horn is the most important.

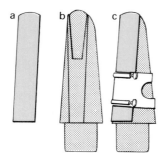

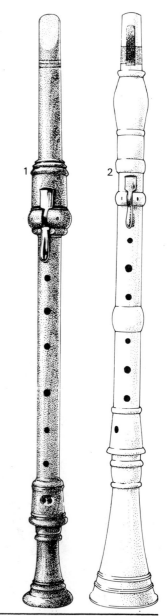

Right Early clarinets with two keys—the other key is on the back, opposite the front key. The clarinet by J. C. Denner (1) is one of his earliest models and is not very different from a chalumeau. Scherer's ivory clarinet of about 1725 (2) shows the shape more typical of later clarinets.

Above Diagrams of the clarinet reed (a), separate mouthpiece (b), and the reed fixed to the mouthpiece by the metal ligature (c). Mouthpieces are usually made of wood or ebonite. Reeds are usually natural cane, but plastic or fiberglass are sometimes used.

1 Two-keyed clarinet, J. C. Denner, early 18th century (Bavarian National Museum, Munich)
2 Two-keyed clarinet, ivory, Scherer, c. 1725

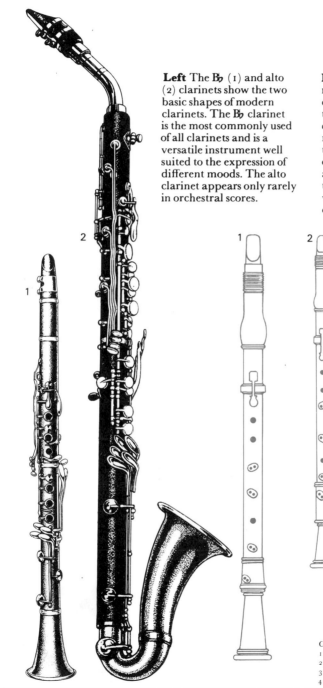

Left The B♭ (1) and alto
(2) clarinets show the two
basic shapes of modern
clarinets. The B♭ clarinet
is the most commonly used
of all clarinets and is a
versatile instrument well
suited to the expression of
different moods. The alto
clarinet appears only rarely
in orchestral scores.

Below Modern
reproductions of a family of
chalumeaux—bass, alto,
tenor, and soprano. The
chalumeau, a simple single-
reed wood instrument, was
the direct ancestor of the
orchestral clarinet. Even
after the development of
the clarinet, chalumeaux
were used in opera
orchestras.

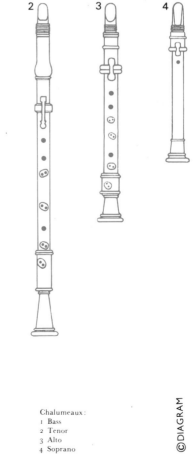

Chalumeaux:
1 Bass
2 Tenor
3 Alto
4 Soprano

©DIAGRAM

Below Modern clarinet family, comprising E♭, B♭, A, alto, bass, and contrabass instruments. The B♭ (2) and A (3) are the most often used, and professional players have matched pairs. The E♭ (1) clarinet is less common and is used for special effects. It appears in Berlioz's Fantastic Symphony.

Right A single-reed version of the tarogato (1) was made by the instrument maker J. V. Schunda in the 1890s. The heckelclarina (2), an obscure and little used member of the clarinet family, dates from the same period.

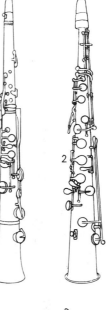

Modern clarinets:
1 E♭
2 B♭
3 A
4 Alto
5 Bass
6 Contrabass

Above Contrabass player. The contrabass clarinet is made in a variety of styles but is seen only very occasionally. It plays extremely low notes and has an easily distinguishable soft, round tone. It is sometimes used in Tchaikovsky's 6th symphony.

©DIAGRAM

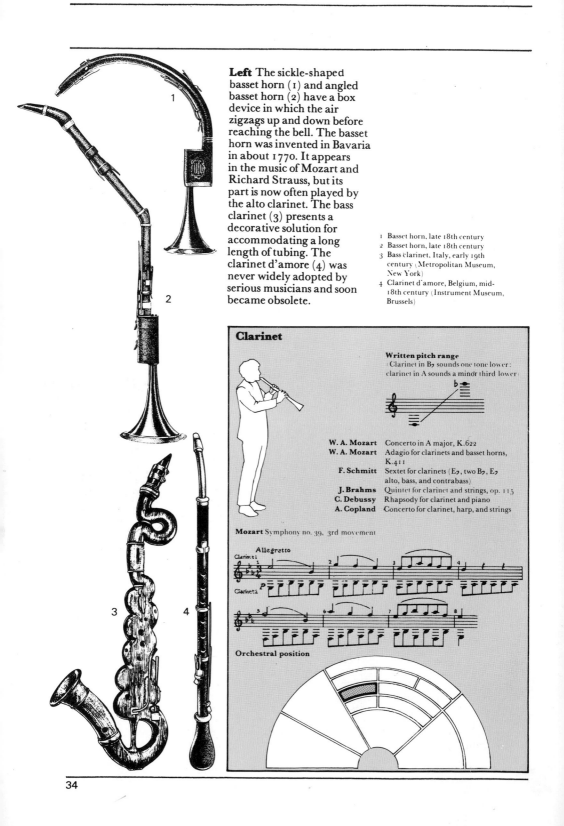

Left The sickle-shaped basset horn (1) and angled basset horn (2) have a box device in which the air zigzags up and down before reaching the bell. The basset horn was invented in Bavaria in about 1770. It appears in the music of Mozart and Richard Strauss, but its part is now often played by the alto clarinet. The bass clarinet (3) presents a decorative solution for accommodating a long length of tubing. The clarinet d'amore (4) was never widely adopted by serious musicians and soon became obsolete.

1 Basset horn, late 18th century
2 Basset horn, late 18th century
3 Bass clarinet, Italy, early 19th century (Metropolitan Museum, New York)
4 Clarinet d'amore, Belgium, mid-18th century (Instrument Museum, Brussels)

Clarinet

Written pitch range
(Clarinet in B♭ sounds one tone lower; clarinet in A sounds a minor third lower)

W. A. Mozart	Concerto in A major, K.622
W. A. Mozart	Adagio for clarinets and basset horns, K.411
F. Schmitt	Sextet for clarinets (E♭, two B♭, E♭ alto, bass, and contrabass)
J. Brahms	Quintet for clarinet and strings, op. 115
C. Debussy	Rhapsody for clarinet and piano
A. Copland	Concerto for clarinet, harp, and strings

Mozart Symphony no. 39, 3rd movement

Allegretto

Clarinet 1

Clarinet 2

Orchestral position

Saxophones

Saxophones are classified with clarinets as members of the single-reed family, but they are actually a hybrid of the clarinet and the oboe. Like the clarinet the saxophone has a single reed attached to a beaked mouthpiece, but its conical tube and flared bell are more typical of the oboe family. The saxophone was invented about 1840 by Adolphe Sax, a Belgian instrument-maker working in Paris. Sax's original family of saxophones comprised 14 members, but only eight of these are normally made today. These eight are, starting with the smallest, the sopranino, soprano, alto, tenor, baritone, bass, contrabass, and subcontrabass. Only the soprano, alto, tenor, and baritone are widely used. Saxophones are regular members of dance bands and military bands, and occasionally they are used to play distinctive solos in orchestral works.

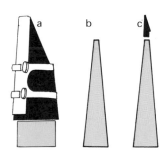

Above Diagram emphasizing the hybrid nature of the saxophone. A single-reed clarinet-type mouthpiece (a) and an instrument with the conical bore typical of the oboe family (b) were brought together (c) to produce an instrument of great versatility.

Right Tenor, or melody, saxophone (1)—with the bent tube and upturned bell characteristic of all but the smallest two members of the saxophone family. Along with the alto and baritone, the tenor saxophone features prominently in the full-bodied sound of the big band. Soprano saxophone (2). Like the smaller sopranino, the soprano saxophone has a straight conical tube. The soprano saxophone is used particularly in jazz bands as a melody instrument along with the clarinet and trumpet. The sopranino is used in military bands.

© DIAGRAM

Bassoons

The bassoon is a bass wind instrument developed during the 17th century from the curtal. It is characterized by two separate parallel tubes joined at one end by a U-tube. Early bassoons had only two keys but in the 19th century German makers experimented with a variety of key mechanisms. Most successful was the system perfected by Heckel and this still remains popular with players all over the world.

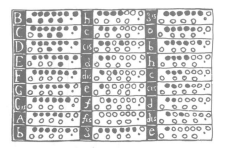

Above An 18th century fingering chart for a four-keyed bassoon. Alternative fingerings were especially important on instruments with only a few keys as a means of correcting inaccurate tuning.

Below Examples of bassoon and contrabassoon reeds. The early 19th century bassoon reed (a) is longer and slimmer than the late 19th century reed (b). The modern bassoon and contrabassoon reeds (c and d) have a squatter profile.

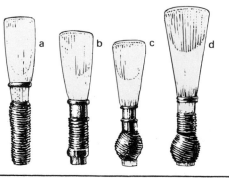

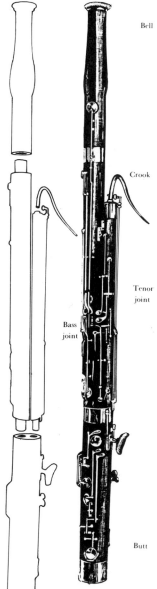

Bell

Crook

Tenor joint

Bass joint

Butt

Above Identification of the parts of a bassoon and a diagram showing how the bassoon is dismantled.

Below Three-keyed bassoon (1) and four-keyed bassoon (2). Made in four sections, these 17th and 18th century instruments had a narrow bore and were played with a large reed. Four-keyed bassoons were used in the orchestra for most of the 18th century, appearing in works by J. S. Bach and Mozart.

1 Three-keyed bassoon, 17th century
2 Four-keyed bassoon, Milhouse, Newark, c.1780
3 Bassoon, Switzerland, 18th century
4 Bassonore, Winnen, Paris, 1844

Below Bassoons with unusual bells. The 18th century Swiss bassoon (3) was used in church. The powerful-toned bassonore (4), invented by Winnen of Paris in the 1830s for military band use, has a wide bore and large bell.

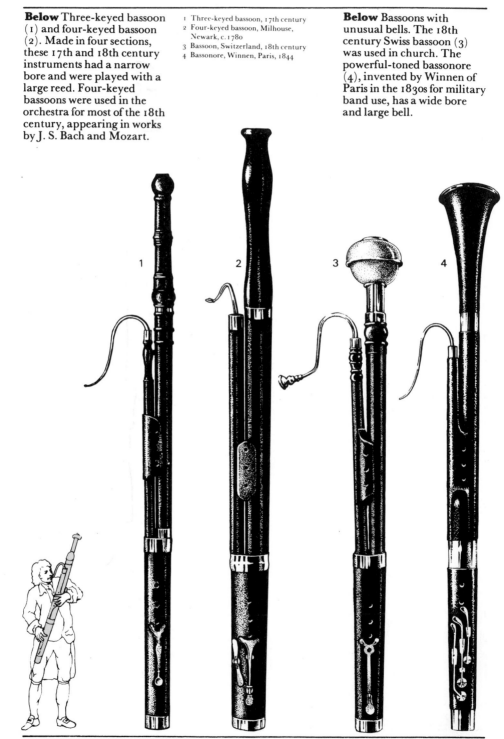

1   2   3   4

Right Modern bassoon—
the lowest sounding regular
member of the orchestral
wind group. The mellow
notes of the bassoon's lower
register provide a firm bass
for orchestral harmony. Its
higher notes, corresponding
to the range of the tenor
voice, are well suited for
solos.

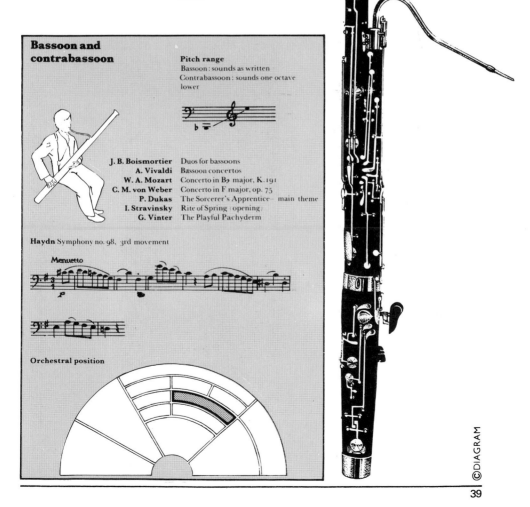

Bassoon and contrabassoon

Pitch range
Bassoon: sounds as written
Contrabassoon: sounds one octave
lower

J. B. Boismortier	Duos for bassoons
A. Vivaldi	Bassoon concertos
W. A. Mozart	Concerto in B♭ major, K.191
C. M. von Weber	Concerto in F major, op. 75
P. Dukas	The Sorcerer's Apprentice— main theme
I. Stravinsky	Rite of Spring (opening)
G. Vinter	The Playful Pachyderm

Haydn Symphony no. 98, 3rd movement

Menuetto

Orchestral position

©DIAGRAM

Above Contrabassoons. The English contrabassoon (1) dates from 1739 and makes an interesting contrast with the modern instrument (2). The contrabassoon plays notes one octave below those of the bassoon but despite its low pitch the sound is rich and gentle.

Horns

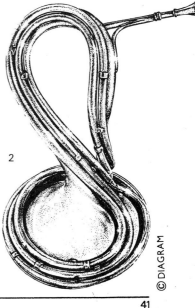

Left 18th century "natural" horn (1) by Ehe (Brussels Conservatoire). These elegant instruments have a narrow cylindrical bore and flaring bell. They were used in the early 18th century orchestra, but their limited melodic range meant that their chief use was to give color to "hunting" passages.

Right An early 19th century Belgian hand horn (2) in the Metropolitan Museum, New York. It has a compact shape and large bell. By placing his hand in the bell the player lowered the pitch of the note played by a semitone, and so increased the total number of available pitches.

© DIAGRAM

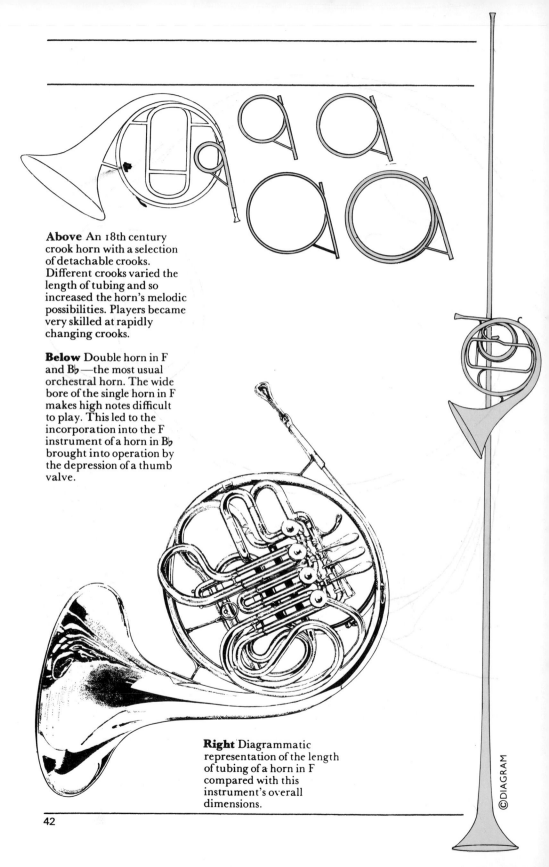

Above An 18th century crook horn with a selection of detachable crooks. Different crooks varied the length of tubing and so increased the horn's melodic possibilities. Players became very skilled at rapidly changing crooks.

Below Double horn in F and B♭ —the most usual orchestral horn. The wide bore of the single horn in F makes high notes difficult to play. This led to the incorporation into the F instrument of a horn in B♭ brought into operation by the depression of a thumb valve.

Right Diagrammatic representation of the length of tubing of a horn in F compared with this instrument's overall dimensions.

©DIAGRAM

WALDHORN.

Es ist nicht leicht ein Fürst der meine Kunst nichtachtet
vielmehr an jeden Hof wird sie aufs höchst geliebt.
wañ man den schüchtern Wild in grünen Wald nachtrachtet
und dem erhitzten Schwein ein kältes Eißen gibt
so wird von meinen Horn das Hertz in Muth gesetzet
auch hält man kein Festin da nicht mein Mund ergötzet.

Left The player supports the horn by placing his right hand in the bell (a). Changing his hand position (b) helps to refine the sound and check imperfections of intonation. The hand can also be used as a mute, to alter a note's pitch, or to achieve different tone color effects.

Right The single horn in F (1) is favored by some players for its simplicity. The Wagner tuba (2) was devised by the composer Richard Wagner for use in "The Ring." Closely related to the horn, Wagner tubas appear in tenor and bass sizes and are played with a horn-type mouthpiece.

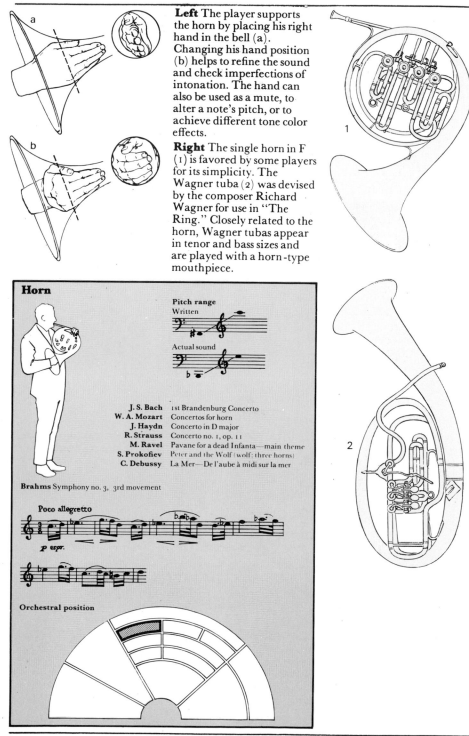

Horn

Pitch range

Written

Actual sound

J. S. Bach	1st Brandenburg Concerto
W. A. Mozart	Concertos for horn
J. Haydn	Concerto in D major
R. Strauss	Concerto no. 1, op. 11
M. Ravel	Pavane for a dead Infanta—main theme
S. Prokofiev	Peter and the Wolf (wolf: three horns)
C. Debussy	La Mer—De l'aube à midi sur la mer

Brahms Symphony no. 3, 3rd movement

Poco allegretto

p espr.

Orchestral position

Trumpets

In the late 18th century makers of brass instruments became particularly interested in the problems of producing a trumpet without the limitations of the "natural" trumpet. A satisfactory solution was found early in the 19th century, when Stölzel and Blühmel produced the first valved trumpets. These trumpets were more versatile and enabled players to play tunes including a far greater range of notes.

1 Slide trumpet, Köhler, London, c.1865 (Horniman Museum, London)
2 Hand trumpet, Sautermeister et Müller, Lyon, c.1820

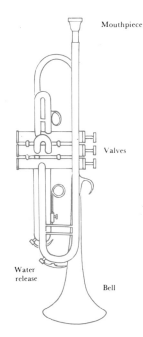

Mouthpiece

Valves

Water release

Bell

1

2

Above Identification of parts of a valved orchestral trumpet.

Left The slide trumpet (1) used the lengthening-tube principle of the trombone. The curved trumpet (2) allowed the hand to be placed in the bell to lower the pitch. Both were superseded by valved instruments.

©DIAGRAM

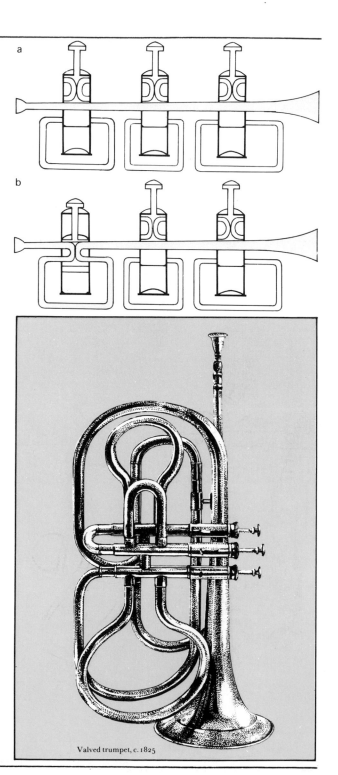

Right Diagrams demonstrating the valve mechanism of a trumpet. When the valve is at rest (a) air passes directly through the main tube. When the valve is depressed (b) the air column is lengthened because air is now diverted through the extra length of tubing.

a

b

Right An early valved trumpet—with Stölzel piston valves. Most valved trumpets have three valves, which may be depressed singly or in any combination. The operation of these valves allows the player to produce all the notes of the scale.

Valved trumpet, c. 1825

Below The modern B♭ trumpet used in orchestras and in jazz, dance, and military bands. Mainly associated with stirring solos, it is also used in the orchestral background texture.

Below The shallow-cup mouthpiece (a) has been replaced by the smaller, deeper mouthpiece (b).

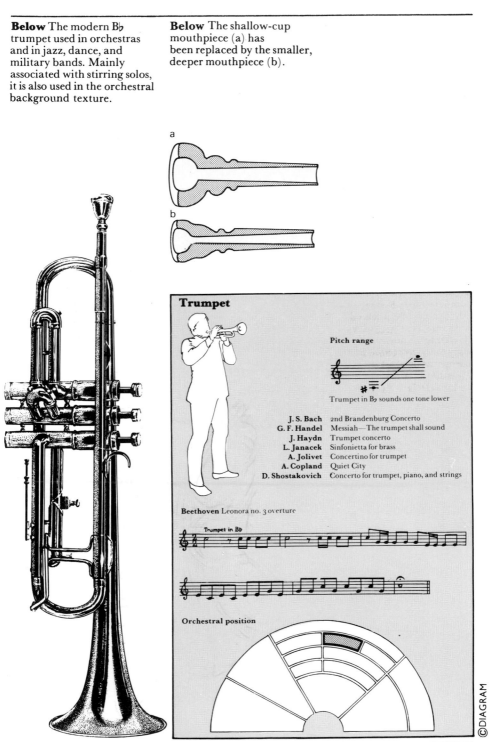

a

b

Trumpet

Pitch range

Trumpet in B♭ sounds one tone lower

J. S. Bach	2nd Brandenburg Concerto
G. F. Handel	Messiah—The trumpet shall sound
J. Haydn	Trumpet concerto
L. Janacek	Sinfonietta for brass
A. Jolivet	Concertino for trumpet
A. Copland	Quiet City
D. Shostakovich	Concerto for trumpet, piano, and strings

Beethoven Leonora no. 3 overture

Trumpet in Bb

Orchestral position

©DIAGRAM

Right Straight (a), cup (b), and wow-wow (c) mutes. Made from wood, metal, rubber, or polystyrene, mutes of many different styles can be fitted into the trumpet's bell to diminish the volume or produce unusual sounds. They are particularly popular with jazz musicians.

a

b

c

Below Unusual modern trumpets (by Getzen). The tilted bell trumpet (1) is sometimes used in jazz bands. The piccolo trumpet (2) plays higher notes than the standard trumpet and is used in military bands. The herald trumpet (3) is a valved version of the renaissance fanfare trumpet.

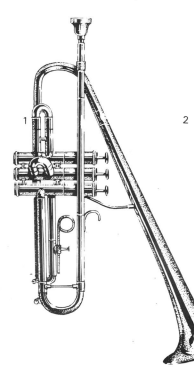

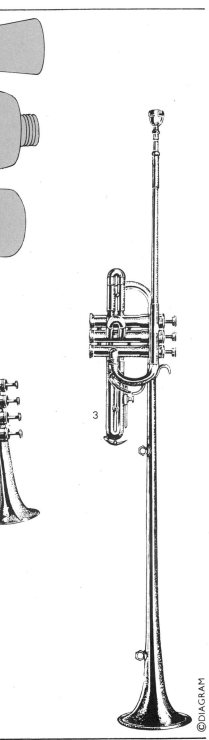

©DIAGRAM

Cornets

The cornet is descended from the post horn. It is usually shaped like a trumpet, but has also been made in a variety of other shapes. In the 1820s it was introduced to the military band, and in the mid-19th century was used in orchestral music by Rossini and Berlioz. Although occasionally found in the orchestra today, the cornet's greatest popularity remains with the military band.

Left The modern cornet includes a substantial amount of cylindrical tubing necessitated by the addition of valves. This makes it different from its "natural" form which is almost completely conical. It is played with a shallow, trumpet-type mouthpiece.

Above A circular cornet — one of the unusual shapes used for this instrument.

Trombones

A trombone is a brass instrument in which the sound is produced by the vibrations of the player's lips. In this respect it is similar to the trumpet, but the trombone is characterized by its telescopic slide used for lengthening the tube. The trombone—then called the sackbut—first appeared in Europe in the 1400s, and still retains its simple basic design. It is popular in orchestras and different types of bands.

Below Diagram showing the effect of moving the trombone's U-shaped slide. The seven playing positions of the slide, in combination with the player's varying breath pressure, determine the pitch of the note sounded.

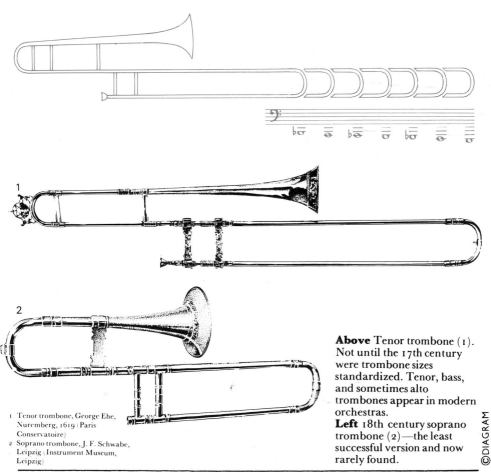

1 Tenor trombone, George Ehe, Nuremberg, 1619 (Paris Conservatoire)
2 Soprano trombone, J. F. Schwabe, Leipzig (Instrument Museum, Leipzig)

Above Tenor trombone (1). Not until the 17th century were trombone sizes standardized. Tenor, bass, and sometimes alto trombones appear in modern orchestras.
Left 18th century soprano trombone (2)—the least successful version and now rarely found.

©DIAGRAM

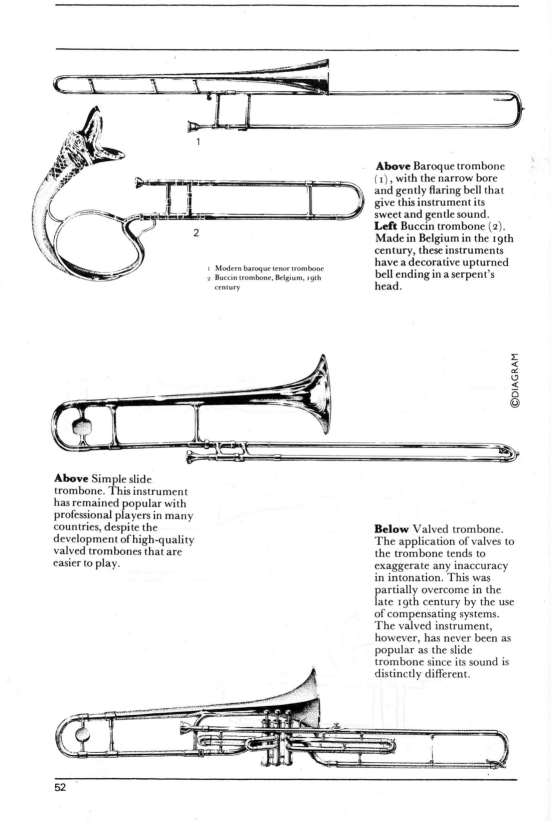

Above Baroque trombone
(1), with the narrow bore
and gently flaring bell that
give this instrument its
sweet and gentle sound.
Left Buccin trombone (2).
Made in Belgium in the 19th
century, these instruments
have a decorative upturned
bell ending in a serpent's
head.

1 Modern baroque tenor trombone
2 Buccin trombone, Belgium, 19th
   century

©DIAGRAM

Above Simple slide
trombone. This instrument
has remained popular with
professional players in many
countries, despite the
development of high-quality
valved trombones that are
easier to play.

Below Valved trombone.
The application of valves to
the trombone tends to
exaggerate any inaccuracy
in intonation. This was
partially overcome in the
late 19th century by the use
of compensating systems.
The valved instrument,
however, has never been as
popular as the slide
trombone since its sound is
distinctly different.

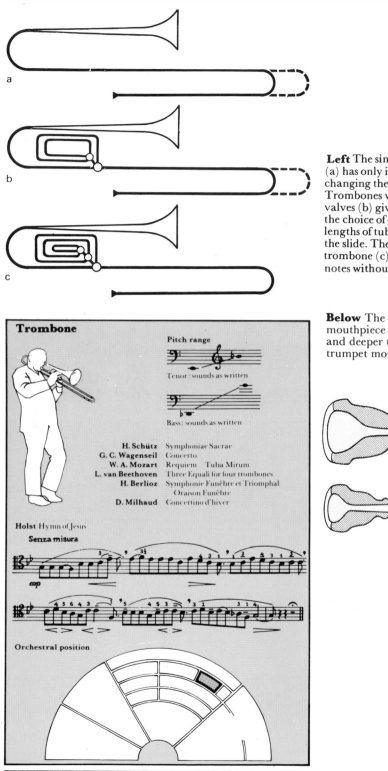

a

b

c

Left The simple trombone (a) has only its slide for changing the pitch of notes. Trombones with one or two valves (b) give the player the choice of different lengths of tubing and retain the slide. The three-valved trombone (c) produces more notes without use of the slide.

Below The trombone mouthpiece (a) is larger and deeper than the trumpet mouthpiece (b).

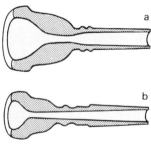

a

b

Trombone

Pitch range

Tenor : sounds as written

Bass : sounds as written

H. Schütz — Symphoniae Sacrae
G. C. Wagenseil — Concerto
W. A. Mozart — Requiem — Tuba Mirum
L. van Beethoven — Three Equali for four trombones
H. Berlioz — Symphonie Funèbre et Triomphal
— Oraison Funèbre
D. Milhaud — Concertino d'hiver

Holst Hymn of Jesus

Senza misura

mp

Orchestral position

Tubas

The tuba is a valved brass instrument with a wide conical bore, flared bell, and cup-shaped mouthpiece. It is characterized by its large size and deep sound. The first tubas were made in the 1830s in Berlin, and the instrument has since appeared in various shapes and sizes. One of these—the E♭ bass tuba—is sometimes called the bombardon. Tubas are used in both the orchestra and the military band.

©DIAGRAM

Above The "recording" tuba —an instrument designed for orchestral recordings. Its forward-pointing bell projects the sound more effectively than the standard upright version.

Below The relative sizes of three modern orchestral tubas —contrabass (a), E♭ bass (b), and F bass (c).

Tuba

Pitch range

Sounds as written

H. Berlioz	Symphonie Fantastique Dies Irae (main theme)
R. Wagner	Götterdämmerung Funeral March
J. Brahms	Tragic Overture

Mussorgsky-Ravel Pictures from an Exhibition

Sempre moderato pesante

PP *poco a poco cresc.*

Orchestral position

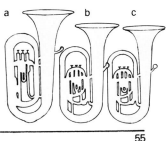

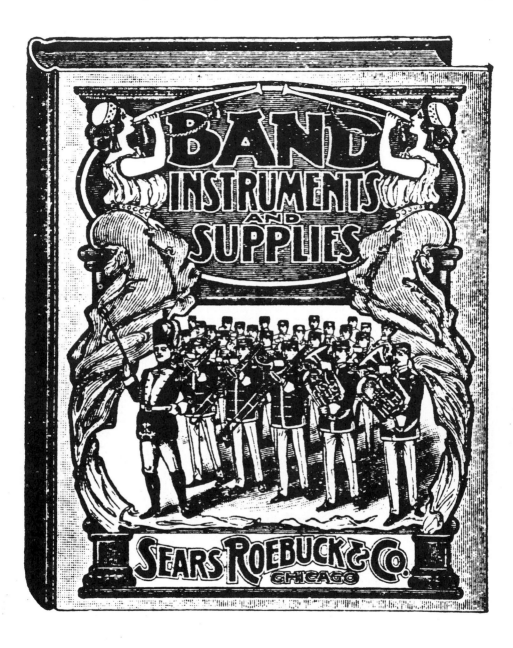

Above The orchestral tuba. The bass member of the brass section of the orchestra, this large instrument is surprisingly agile for its size. Invented in the 1820s, it was uncommon before the 1850s. It is at its most effective when playing quick staccato solos, but is equally capable of playing sustained melodies.

Above The euphonium—a large bugle with three to five valves, said to have been invented in 1843 by Sommer of Weimar. First used to replace the bassoon in the military bands of Russia and Germany, it is now most commonly played in the United States.

©DIAGRAM

Membranophones: introduction

Membranophones are instruments in which the sound is made by the vibration of a stretched membrane, or skin. There are two basic types — drums and, much less important, mirlitons. Evidence from art proves the existence of drums at least 4000 years ago in Mesopotamia and Egypt, but the perishable nature of the materials from which drums are made has meant that few ancient examples survive. Today, drums are enormously popular throughout the world, and are made in a great variety of styles. Many peoples consider drums to have magical and ritual significance, using them to ward off evil and to appeal to good spirits. Drums are also important signaling and battle instruments, as well as being popular for accompanying singing and dancing. Since the 1700s drums have been included in the Western orchestra.

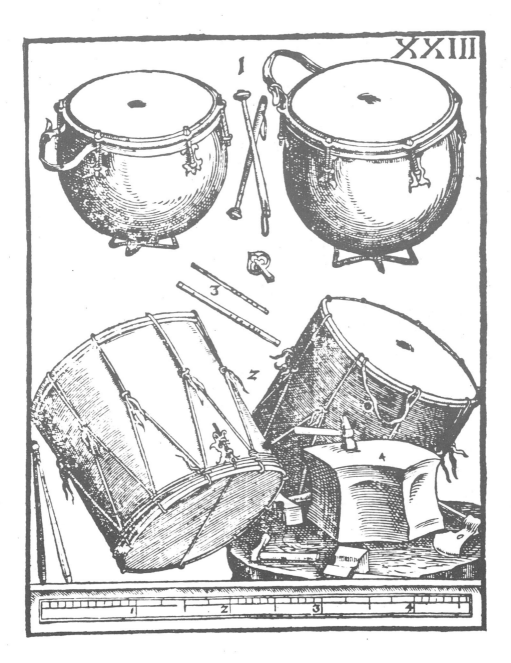

Below Membranophones family tree. There are two basic types of membranophone: drums and mirlitons. Drums may be divided according to shape into tubular, vessel, and frame drums, while a separate category is devoted to drums sounded by friction. Tubular drums include cylindrical, conical, barrel, waisted, goblet, footed, and long drums.

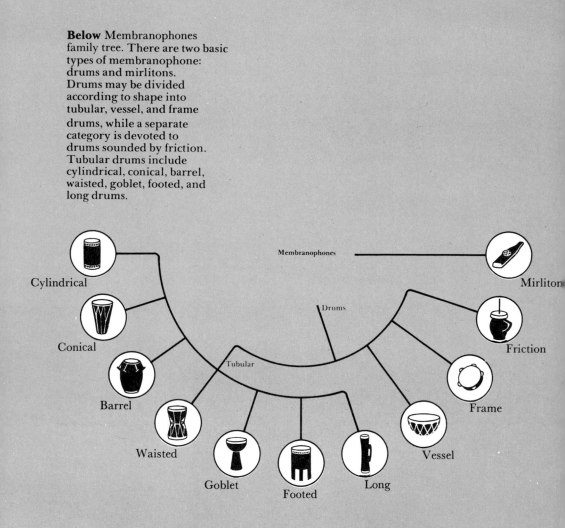

Cylindrical

Conical

Barrel

Waisted

Goblet

Footed

Long

Vessel

Frame

Friction

Mirliton

Membranophones

Drums

Tubular

Below Body shapes. Membranophones are classified by body shape. Cylindrical drums (a) are straight-sided. Conical drums (b) have sloping sides while barrel drums (c) have bulging sides. Waisted or hourglass drums (d) and goblet drums (e) are more elaborate shapes. Footed drums (f) have legs that are usually cut from the drum body. Long drums (g) are made in a variety of shapes but length is a useful distinguishing feature. In frame drums (h) the skin is stretched over a frame. Kettledrums (i) have a vessel or pot body and a single playing head.

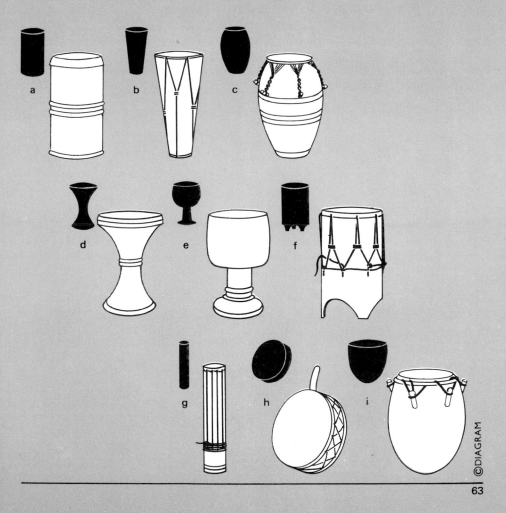

©DIAGRAM

Below Vibrating membranes. In a membranophone sound is produced by the vibration of a stretched membrane. There are two types of membranophone: drums (a) and mirlitons (b). A mirliton is sounded by blowing or humming into the instrument.

a

b

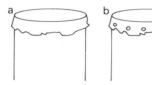

Above Skin attachment. The membrane, or skin, may be attached in five different ways. It may be glued (a), nailed (b), pegged (c), laced (d), or lapped on a hoop (e).

Below Lacing. Different styles of lacing are employed for attaching drum skins. Common patterns are N lacing (a), W lacing (b), X lacing (c), Y lacing (d), or net lacing (e).

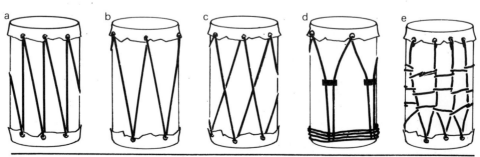

Below Sounding a drum. The skin is vibrated by beating with hands (a), sticks (b), beaters (c), or wire brushes (d). The skins of the clapper drum (e) are struck with small beads as the drum is shaken. Some friction drums are sounded by a stick piercing the skin (f).

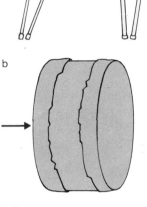

Above Playing heads. Drums may be single-headed with only one skin (a), or double-headed with a skin at each end. Double-headed drums may be played on one head (b), or on both heads (c).

Below Tuning. Drums are tuned by altering the tension of the skin—by adjusting the lacing (a), moving chocs under the lacing (b), or turning keys or taps (c). Tone quality may be changed by applying small sticky balls (1) or paste (2 and 3) to the playing head.

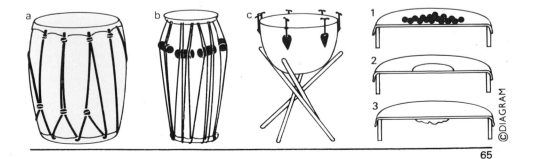

©DIAGRAM

Drums

Drums play an important part in the "percussion" section of Western orchestras and bands. The art and literature of ancient times show that drums were used by all the major civilizations of the past, but the perishable nature of the materials from which most drums are made has meant that few ancient examples survive. Drums had a major role in the music of medieval and renaissance Europe. Especially common were the tabor and side drum, which are still played today. Also common in medieval times were nakers, small kettledrums of Arabic origin that survive as the modern orchestral timpani. In addition to the timpani—most important because they are tuned to specific pitches—the basic orchestral drum group consists of side, tenor, and bass drums. In modern dance bands drums of Latin American origin play an increasingly significant role.

1 Drum head
2 Tuning gauge
3 Shell
4 Struts
5 "Crown"
6 Pedal

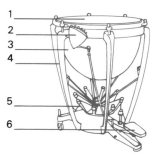

1
2
3
4
5
6

Above Identification of parts of a modern timpanum. The tuning is controlled by a pedal which alters the skin tension by means of rods and "crown" mechanism. A tuning gauge worked by the pedal indicates the pitch.
Left Modern orchestral timpanum (Premier).

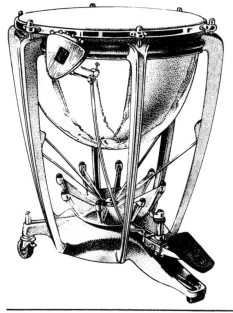

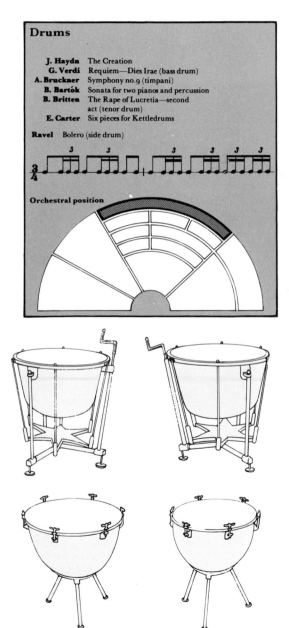

Drums

J. Haydn The Creation
G. Verdi Requiem—Dies Irae (bass drum)
A. Bruckner Symphony no.9 (timpani)
B. Bartók Sonata for two pianos and percussion
B. Britten The Rape of Lucretia—second act (tenor drum)
E. Carter Six pieces for Kettledrums

Ravel Bolero (side drum)

Orchestral position

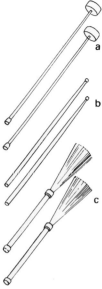

Above Timpani sticks (a), side drum sticks (b), and wire brushes used for special effects (c).

Left 19th century machine timpani. Developed to reduce the amount of time needed for tuning, these instruments were tuned with a single handle. Turning the handle operated a mechanism for turning all the screws at once, so ensuring equal tension at all points on the drum head.

Left Modern hand-screw timpani. Despite the advantages of modern tuning mechanisms these simpler, cheaper drums are still very popular. Although impracticable for most modern music, they are useful for earlier music requiring only three or four different pitches.

© DIAGRAM

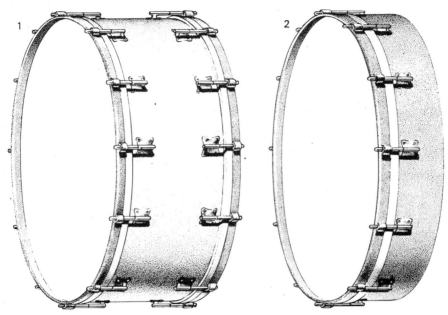

Above and right Modern orchestral drums. The double-headed bass drum (1) and single-headed gong drum (2) are played with large padded beaters. The side drum (3) is usually fitted with snares—eight or more lengths of gut, nylon, or wire stretched over the lower head to give extra brilliance to the sound. The side drum and the tenor drum (4) are played with hard wood sticks. The tambourine (5) may be shaken, struck, or, less commonly, sounded by friction.

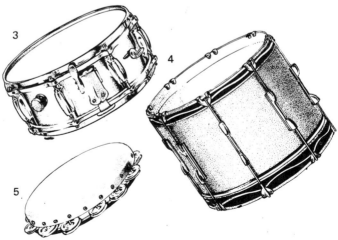

3

Idiophones: introduction

Idiophones are instruments made of naturally
sonorous material, sounded in a variety of
different ways. Their development began many
thousands of years ago when early man first
clashed together sticks, stones, and bones to
emphasize the rhythms of his clapping hands and
stamping feet. Similar primitive idiophones
made of natural materials are today used by
many peoples to accompany singing and dancing
and to act as signaling instruments. Interest in
the different sounds and pitches produced by
objects of varying sizes and materials led to the
development of such instruments as the
xylophone and gong chime. The Western
symphony orchestra includes a wide variety of
"percussion" instruments, ranging from the
simple wood block to tuned instruments like the
tubular bells and glockenspiel.

Below Idiophones family tree. There are eight basic types of idiophone: stamping, stamped, shaken, percussion, concussion, friction, scraped, and plucked. The largest group —percussion idiophones— has a major subdivision according to shape.

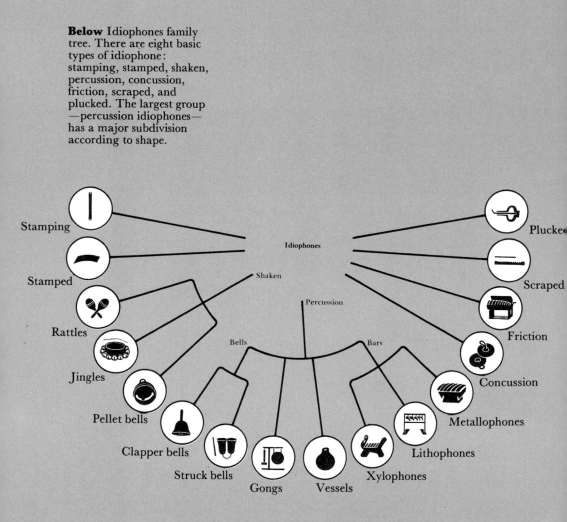

Stamping

Stamped

Rattles

Jingles

Pellet bells

Clapper bells

Struck bells

Gongs

Vessels

Xylophones

Lithophones

Metallophones

Concussion

Friction

Scraped

Plucked

Idiophones

Shaken

Percussion

Bells

Bars

Below and right Shapes.
Idiophones are found in
many shapes. Common
examples include the
stamping stick (a), bells
(b), gongs (c), vessels (d),
and bar idiophones like the
xylophone (e). Along with
material and sounding
method, shape affects the
type of sound produced.

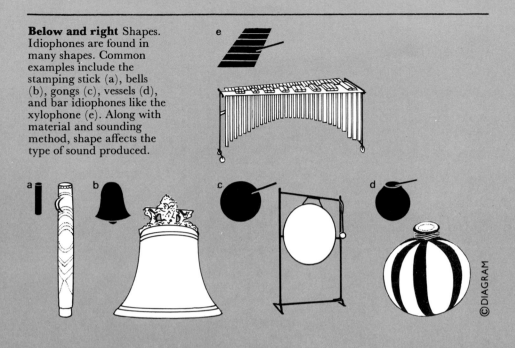

©DIAGRAM

Right and below
Sounding. Idiophones are
classified according to how
the sound is produced. The
eight basic sounding
methods are illustrated
below: stamping (a),
stamped (b), shaken (c),
percussion (d), concussion
(e), friction (f), scraped
(g), and plucked (h).

75

Right Stamping idiophones are instruments sounded by banging them on the ground or another hard surface. They include sticks, tubes, and tap shoes.

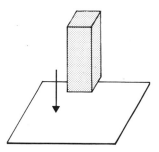

Left Stamped idiophones. In this case the sound comes from the surface on which the stamping takes place. Stamped pits and boards are good examples.

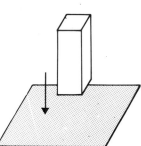

Right Percussion idiophones. Also called struck idiophones, these instruments are made to sound by striking them with a stick or beater. Gongs and xylophones are characteristic examples.

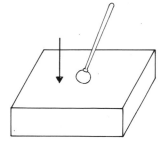

Left Shaken idiophones. Of the instruments sounded by shaking, rattles and jingles are two common types. They are made from many different materials in a great variety of styles.

Right Concussion idiophones. An idiophone that produces sound when two or more similar parts hit together is called a concussion idiophone. Examples are cymbals and clappers.

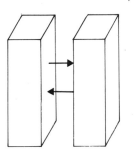

Left Friction idiophones are instruments sounded by rubbing. Sometimes, as with the musical saw, two objects are rubbed together. Other instruments, such as musical glasses, are rubbed with a moistened finger.

Right Scraped idiophones. These instruments have a notched or ridged surface, and produce a series of short taps when a stick is drawn over them. Examples include bone scrapers and the washboard.

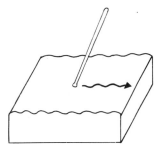

Left Plucked idiophones. Also called linguaphones, these instruments have one or more flexible tongues attached to a frame. They are sounded by plucking the tongues. Jew's harps and sansas are examples.

©DIAGRAM

Percussion

The percussion section of the modern orchestra includes two basic types of instrument. The simplest type, including the triangle and wood block, are untuned and produce a note of indeterminate pitch. Tuned instruments, including the xylophone and tubular bells, are capable of playing melodies. The history of the orchestral percussion group dates from the mid-18th century when an interest in Turkish—or "Janissary"—music first led to the introduction of such instruments as the cymbals and triangle to supplement the drum section. In the 19th century sophisticated tuned instruments including the xylophone and tubular bells began to appear in the scores of Tchaikovsky and Saint-Saëns. More recently composers like Benjamin Britten have called for a variety of "sound makers" for special effects, including slung mugs struck with wood spoons, cog rattles, and "whips."

Right Wood blocks and triangle. The tulip block (1) and the two-tone block (3) are less common versions of the "Chinese" block (2). All are tapped sharply with a hard wood beater to give a penetrating sound. The metal triangle (4) is among the most important of the orchestral percussion instruments.

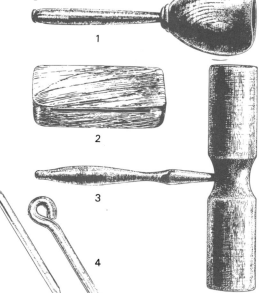

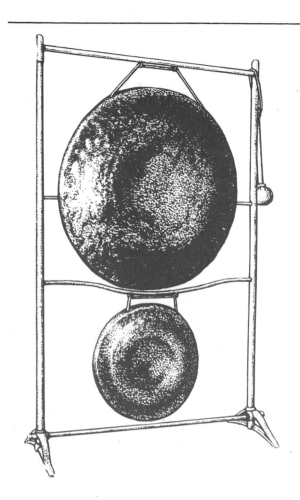

Left Orchestral tam-tams. These bronze gongs, made in a variety of sizes, from 2ft to 5ft in diameter, are suspended in a frame and struck with a soft beater.

Above Cymbal playing methods—clashing two cymbals together (a) and striking a single cymbal with a beater (b).
Below Modern orchestral marimba. Taking its name from a folk instrument of Africa and Central America, the orchestral marimba is a deep version of the orchestral xylophone. The pitch range of marimbas varies from three to five octaves. Some smaller versions are called xylorimbas.

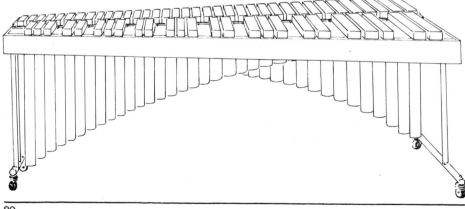

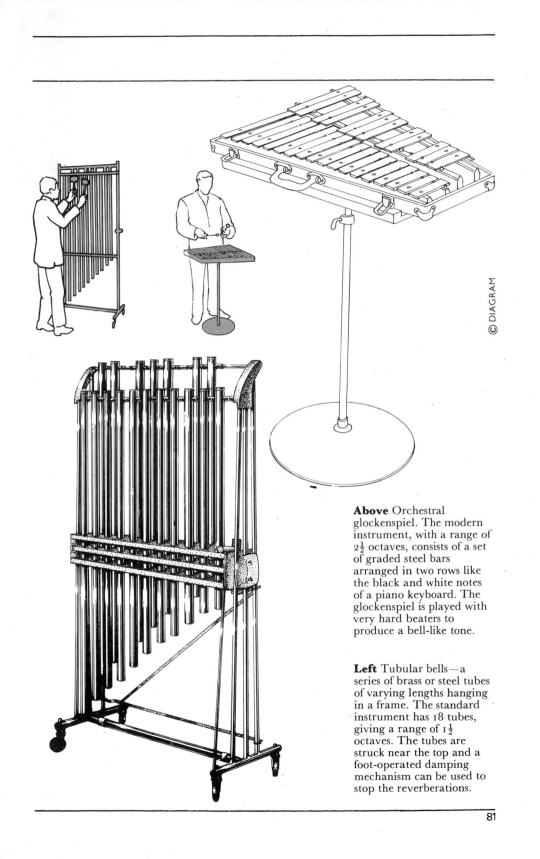

© DIAGRAM

Above Orchestral
glockenspiel. The modern
instrument, with a range of
$2\frac{1}{2}$ octaves, consists of a set
of graded steel bars
arranged in two rows like
the black and white notes
of a piano keyboard. The
glockenspiel is played with
very hard beaters to
produce a bell-like tone.

Left Tubular bells—a
series of brass or steel tubes
of varying lengths hanging
in a frame. The standard
instrument has 18 tubes,
giving a range of $1\frac{1}{2}$
octaves. The tubes are
struck near the top and a
foot-operated damping
mechanism can be used to
stop the reverberations.

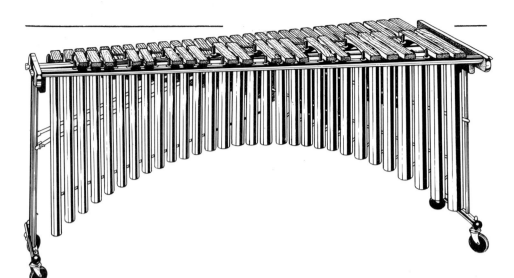

Above Modern orchestral xylophone—the most important tuned percussion instrument, consisting of two rows of wood bars suspended over hollow tube resonators. The commonest orchestral versions have a range of $3\frac{1}{2}$ or 4 octaves, and may be struck with different types of beaters.

Percussion

C. Saint-Saëns	Danse Macabre (xylophone)
P. Tchaikovsky	1812 Overture (tubular bells)
P. Dukas	The Sorcerer's Apprentice (glockenspiel)
D. Milhaud	Concerto for marimba, vibraphone and orchestra
B. Bartók	Sonata for two pianos and percussion
W. Walton	Façade (wood block)
O. Messiaen	Et Exspecto Resurrectionem Mortuorum (cow bells)

Tchaikovsky Nutcracker Suite, Sugar Plum Fairy (celeste)

Bizet Carmen (castanets)

Orchestral position

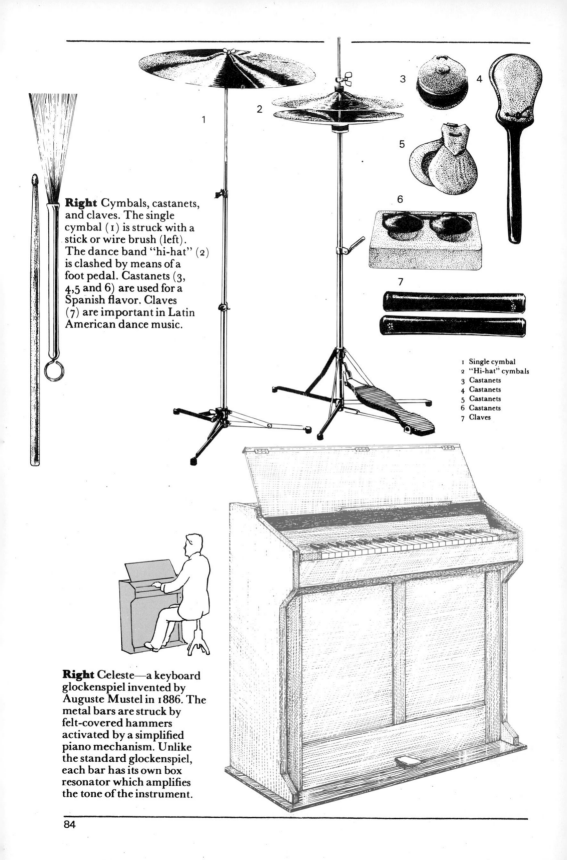

Right Cymbals, castanets, and claves. The single cymbal (1) is struck with a stick or wire brush (left). The dance band "hi-hat" (2) is clashed by means of a foot pedal. Castanets (3, 4, 5 and 6) are used for a Spanish flavor. Claves (7) are important in Latin American dance music.

1 Single cymbal
2 "Hi-hat" cymbals
3 Castanets
4 Castanets
5 Castanets
6 Castanets
7 Claves

Right Celeste—a keyboard glockenspiel invented by Auguste Mustel in 1886. The metal bars are struck by felt-covered hammers activated by a simplified piano mechanism. Unlike the standard glockenspiel, each bar has its own box resonator which amplifies the tone of the instrument.

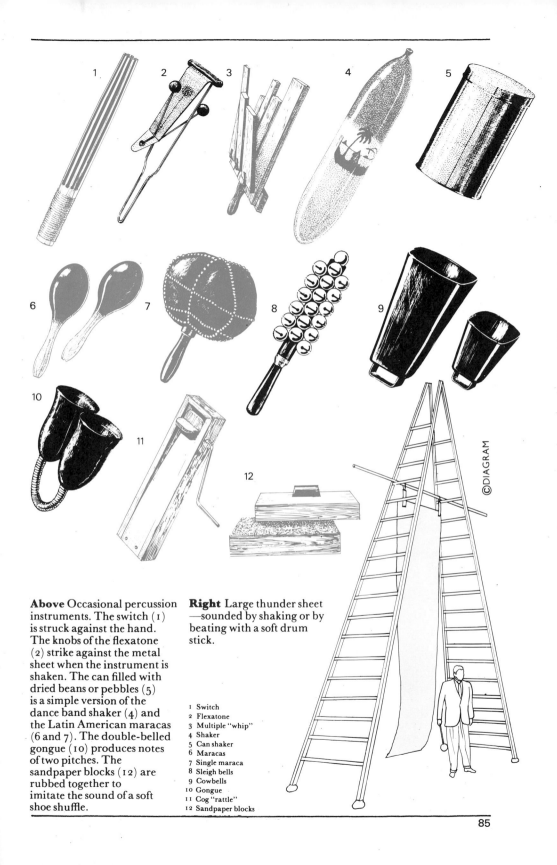

Above Occasional percussion instruments. The switch (1) is struck against the hand. The knobs of the flexatone (2) strike against the metal sheet when the instrument is shaken. The can filled with dried beans or pebbles (5) is a simple version of the dance band shaker (4) and the Latin American maracas (6 and 7). The double-belled gongue (10) produces notes of two pitches. The sandpaper blocks (12) are rubbed together to imitate the sound of a soft shoe shuffle.

Right Large thunder sheet —sounded by shaking or by beating with a soft drum stick.

1 Switch
2 Flexatone
3 Multiple "whip"
4 Shaker
5 Can shaker
6 Maracas
7 Single maraca
8 Sleigh bells
9 Cowbells
10 Gongue
11 Cog "rattle"
12 Sandpaper blocks

©DIAGRAM

85

Chordophones: introduction

Chordophones are instruments in which the sound is made by the vibration of strings. There are five basic types: bows, lyres, harps, lutes, and zithers. Of these, the oldest and simplest is the musical bow which is still common in Africa and the Americas. Harps and lyres both appeared about 5000 years ago in ancient Egypt and Sumeria. The harp survives in many parts of the world, although the lyre is now confined almost exclusively to Africa. Plucked lutes also have a long history and are among the most popular of all folk instruments. The bow was first applied to the lute in the 10th century AD, and from these early bowed lutes developed the members of the modern violin family. Zithers appear in a wide variety of styles, ranging from simple tube zithers to the sophisticated keyboard instruments of Western Europe.

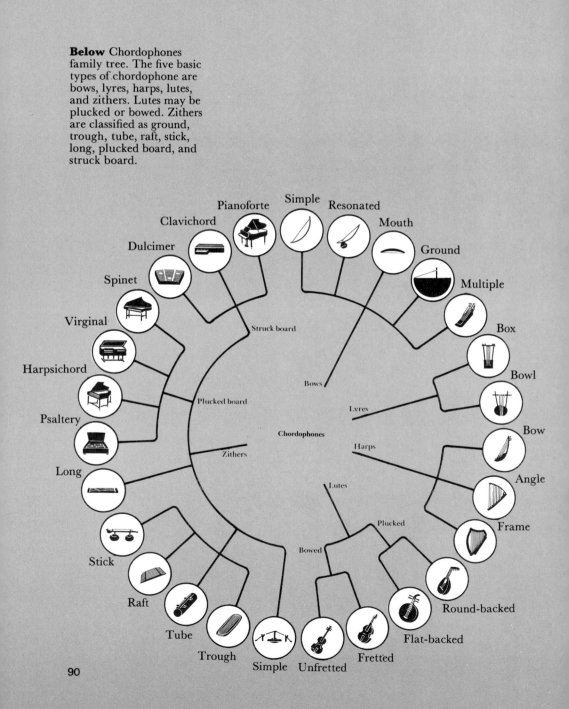

Below Chordophones family tree. The five basic types of chordophone are bows, lyres, harps, lutes, and zithers. Lutes may be plucked or bowed. Zithers are classified as ground, trough, tube, raft, stick, long, plucked board, and struck board.

Simple
Pianoforte
Clavichord
Resonated
Dulcimer
Mouth
Spinet
Ground
Virginal
Multiple
Harpsichord
Box
Psaltery
Bowl
Long
Bow
Stick
Angle
Raft
Frame
Tube
Round-backed
Trough
Flat-backed
Simple
Fretted
Unfretted

Struck board
Bows
Plucked board
Lyres
Chordophones
Zithers
Harps
Lutes
Plucked
Bowed

Below Stringing. The relationship of the strings to the body or resonator provides the usual means of classifying chordophones. The musical bow (a) has one or more strings attached to each end of a curved stick. The strings of the lyre (b) run from a resonator to a crossbar supported by two arms.

Harp strings run at an oblique angle from the resonator to the neck (c). Instruments of the lute family have strings running from near the base of the body, over a bridge, to the end of the neck (d). Zither strings (e), raised by bridges, run along the instrument's length parallel to the body.

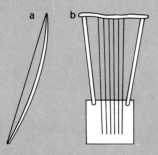
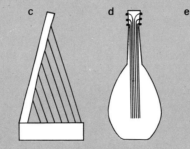

Below Lifting the strings. To vibrate freely the strings of lyres, lutes, and zithers must be lifted from the body. On some instruments the strings are attached to the body and then pass over a bridge (a); other examples have a string holder which also acts as a bridge (b).

Below String attachment. Different methods are used for attaching strings to a chordophone's neck. In some primitive examples the string is tied direct to the neck (a). Instruments are easier to tune if the strings are tied to a tuning ring (b) or fastened to a peg (c).

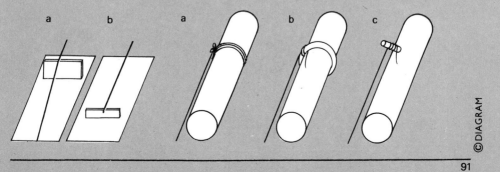

Below Sounding the strings.
Of playing methods used
for chordophones, the most
common are plucking—
with the fingers (a) or a
plectrum (b)—and bowing
(c). Some zithers are
played with beaters or
hammers (d) while the
strings of the aeolian harp
(e) are sounded by the
wind.

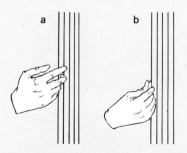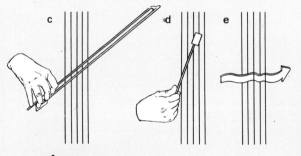

Right How a string
vibrates. An activated
string vibrates not only as a
whole but also in sections as
shown in the diagram. The
primary, or longest,
vibration determines the
pitch produced. This pitch
is called the fundamental.
Secondary vibrations
produce harmonics or
overtones—pitches which
sound in conjunction with
the fundamental. The
presence of different
harmonics gives each
instrument its own tone
color. By touching a string
very lightly with his finger
while bowing it normally,
the player obtains a
harmonic in place of the
fundamental.

Right Strings and pitch. Pitch is affected by a string's length, tension, and thickness. A short string gives a higher pitch than a long one (a). A string at high tension gives a higher pitch than a less taut string (b). A thin string gives a higher pitch than a thick one (c).

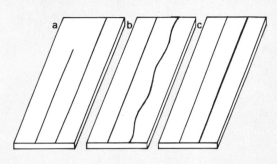

Right Resonators. An activated string gives a better tone if the instrument has a soundbox, or resonator. String vibrations are transferred to the resonator which reinforces and amplifies the tone. Devices like the violin soundpost help spread the vibrations (right).

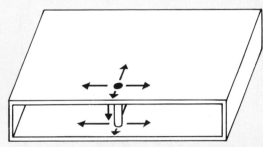

Right Raising the pitch. A higher pitch may be obtained from a string by shortening its vibrating length. In performance this is usually achieved by "stopping" the string— pressing it against the neck or body of the instrument— usually with the finger (a). Some instruments have frets—very low bridges on the neck or body—which show the player where the string should be stopped (b). Many zithers have movable bridges which can be adjusted to give the string a particular vibrating length and thus a particular pitch (c).

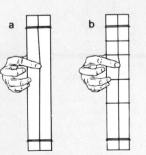

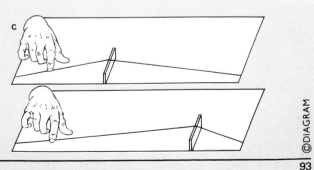

Violins

The violin is probably the best known of all Western orchestral instruments. It is the smallest member of the family of bowed stringed instruments that includes the viola, violoncello, and double bass. The violin emerged around 1550 from the medieval fiddle, the rebec, and the lira da braccio, though details of the transition are confused. The early violin proper, however, had four strings, lateral pegs, a waisted body, and f-shaped sound holes—a form that has changed little in 400 years. Violin making began in 16th century Italy and later flourished under makers such as Stradivari and Guarneri. During the 18th century, violinist-composers such as Vivaldi and Tartini expanded the scope of the playing technique, and the perfecting of the bow in the 19th century further increased the possibilities of this most versatile instrument.

Below Violin bows. The bow pioneered by Corelli around 1700 was short and inelastic (a). Tartini's bow of 50 years later was longer and more flexible (b). The Tourte bow, developed in the 19th century and still used today, has an inward-curving stick designed for good balance (c).

Right Interior of a violin. The soundpost (a), set under the right foot of the bridge, transmits vibrations to the back of the violin. The bass bar (b), glued to the back of the belly, stiffens the body and distributes the vibrations. Without these devices, resonance is reduced and the tone muffled.

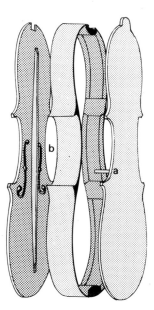

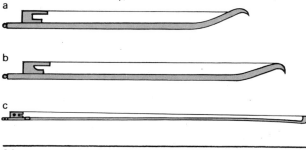

a

b

c

Left Pizzicato action. Sometimes the player is required to pluck the string with the forefinger of the right hand, so producing a guitar-like effect. Paganini, the 19th century violinist and composer, introduced the virtuoso technique of plucking the strings with the left hand.

Below The Greffuhle violin. Made in 1709, it is a fine example of the craftsmanship of Antonio Stradivari. The ribs and scroll are decorated with delicate inlay work.

a

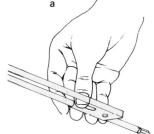

b

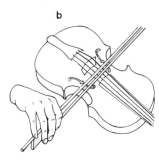

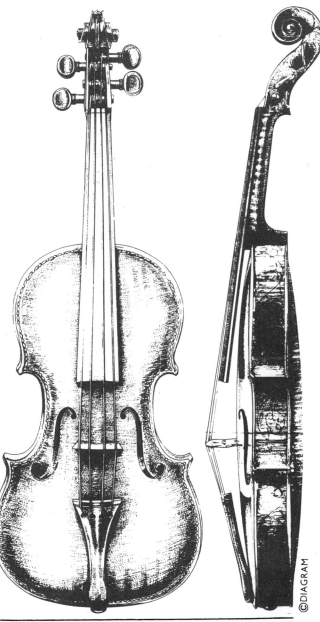

Above Holding the bow (a) and bowing position (b). The thumb, slightly bent, is inserted between the stick and the hair, close to the nut and opposite the first and second fingers. Different effects can be achieved by varying the method of bowing. The commonest method consists of smooth down-strokes and up-strokes, in which the bow is drawn across the string from nut to point and back again. Other bowing methods include staccato or detached strokes, "hammered" strokes where each stroke is released forcefully, and "jeté" strokes where the bow is allowed to bounce across the strings.

©DIAGRAM

Right Modern violin. The demand in the 18th and 19th centuries for a fuller, more brilliant tone led to improvements which have been retained to the present day. These include strings that are thinner and at greater tension, and a higher, more curved bridge that facilitates clean bowing.

© DIAGRAM

Above Violin mute—used for softening the tone. The mute is a comb-like device with three prongs. Clamped over the bridge, it limits the vibrations of the bridge and gives a quiet, nasal tone.

Below A comparison of the size of the violin (a) with the larger members of its family—the viola (b), the violoncello (c), and the double bass (d).

Below Diagram showing the parts of a modern violin and bow.

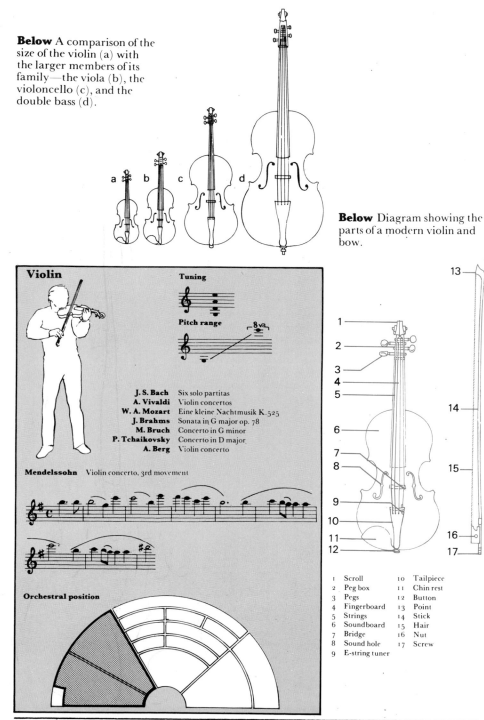

Violin

Tuning

Pitch range

J. S. Bach	Six solo partitas
A. Vivaldi	Violin concertos
W. A. Mozart	Eine kleine Nachtmusik K.525
J. Brahms	Sonata in G major op. 78
M. Bruch	Concerto in G minor
P. Tchaikovsky	Concerto in D major
A. Berg	Violin concerto

Mendelssohn Violin concerto, 3rd movement

Orchestral position

1	Scroll	10	Tailpiece
2	Peg box	11	Chin rest
3	Pegs	12	Button
4	Fingerboard	13	Point
5	Strings	14	Stick
6	Soundboard	15	Hair
7	Bridge	16	Nut
8	Sound hole	17	Screw
9	E-string tuner		

Violas

The viola is the alto member of the bowed string family and much of its history is shared with the violin. Structurally identical to the violin, though slightly larger, the viola was long overshadowed by the greater technical convenience of the smaller instrument. From the late 1700s composers began to exploit the viola's characteristically mellow tone color, and gave it at last some of the importance it deserves.

Below Unusual violas. The viola in the shape of an early fiddle (1) has sloping shoulders reminiscent of the viol. It dates from the 18th century and is probably French. The guitar-shaped viola (2), based on a type devised by Chanot, was made in Paris around 1825.

Right Modern viola. The size of the viola varies from 16–18in; a larger body gives a fuller tone but is more unwieldy in playing. This century has seen the first virtuoso viola players—such as Lionel Tertis and William Primrose—who have done much to increase the instrument's importance.

1

2

© DIAGRAM

Musikalischer Spaß

für

zwei Violinen, Bratsche, zwei Hörner u. Baß

geschrieben in Wien den 14ten Juny 1787

von

W. A. MOZART.

93tes Werk.

Nach dem Originalmanuscripte des Autors herausgegeben

Nº 1508.   Preis f 2.

Offenbach a/m, bei J. André.

Left Comparative sizes of the viola and violin. The approximate body length of the viola is 17in—about 3in longer than the violin. In relation to the violin, the viola is proportionately small for its pitch—in theory it should be half as long again as the violin.

Below 18th century viola player. In its early history, the viola enjoyed less importance than the violin in the string texture. Works such as Bach's 3rd and 6th Brandenburg concertos, and the later quartets of Haydn and Mozart, gave the viola an interesting and often difficult part to play.

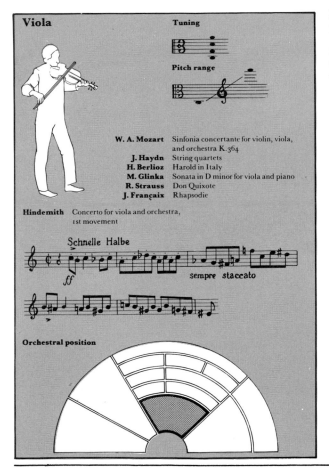

Viola

Tuning

Pitch range

W. A. Mozart	Sinfonia concertante for violin, viola, and orchestra K.364
J. Haydn	String quartets
H. Berlioz	Harold in Italy
M. Glinka	Sonata in D minor for viola and piano
R. Strauss	Don Quixote
J. Françaix	Rhapsodie

Hindemith Concerto for viola and orchestra, 1st movement

Schnelle Halbe

ff

sempre staccato

Orchestral position

Violoncellos

The violoncello, popularly called the cello, is the bass member of the violin family. It is played with a bow shorter and thicker than that of the violin, and is fitted with a retractable spike for resting on the floor. Developed in the 1500s, the cello existed for almost 150 years alongside the tenor viola da gamba whose popularity was slow to fade. From the 1700s the cello became a favorite solo instrument.

Right Modern cello. Despite its comparatively large size the cello is one of the most versatile and expressive of all instruments. Good resonance is assured by its large body which is proportionately deeper than that of the violin. It is equally effective in both solo and accompanying passages.

Right Comparison of piccolo and full size cellos. The piccolo was a small 18th century version of the standard cello. Intended for solo use, it was tuned like the standard cello although occasionally an extra treble string was added. It appears in some of the cantatas of J. S. Bach.

Below 18th century continuo player. The baroque cellist was important in both the orchestra and the chamber group. He provided, in conjunction with an organ or harpsichord, a bass line to act as a firm foundation for the instrumental harmonies. This technique was called continuo playing.

Violoncello

Tuning

Pitch range

J. S. Bach	Six suites for solo cello
J. Haydn	Cello concerto in C major
J. Brahms	Sonata in E minor op. 38
A. Dvorak	Cello concerto
C. Saint-Saëns	The Swan
B. Britten	Cello Symphony
K. Penderecki	Sonata for cello and orchestra

Wagner Siegfried Idyll

Ruhig bewegt

P dolce

più P

Orchestral position

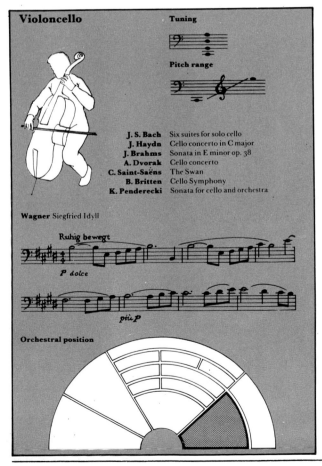

VIOLON

Wann dorten Padua. mit seiner Gambe pranget
so leist ich beßre dienst mit meinem Violon.
ich hab mit dieser Kunst unsterblichs Lob erlanget,
und heiß mit allem Recht ein wahrer Musen-Sohn:
weil meine Saiten selbst am Helicon erthönen.
wird einst Apollo noch die muntre Scheitel krönen.

Double basses

The double bass, the deepest member of the violin family, was developed in the 1500s from the violone, the double bass viol. Experiments with body size and number of strings were made in an attempt to simplify the playing technique. Two important types of bow are now in use—the French bow, held "overhand" like the violin bow, and the Simandl bow, named after its inventor, which is held like the viol bow with the palm up.

Double bass

Tuning

Sounds one octave lower

Pitch range

Sounds one octave lower

L. Boccherini	String quintet
F. Schubert	Trout quintet for piano and strings
L. van Beethoven	Septet op. 20
L. Spohr	Nonet op. 31
R. Strauss	Also sprach Zarathustra
E. Varèse	Octandre

Strauss Ein Heldenleben

Lebhaft bewegt

Orchestral position

Below 18th century double bass player. The size of the instrument meant that the player had to stand up in order to reach it comfortably. Most modern players sit on the edge of a stool to play.

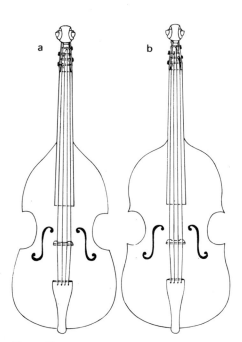

a

b

Above Two common double bass designs. The instrument with sloping shoulders (a), based on the shape of the earlier viola da gamba, is a typical German design of the 18th century. The violin-shaped design (b) was favored by Italian makers. Instruments of both designs are still played today.

Right Modern double bass. The average double bass played in orchestras and bands is just over 6ft high. Most instruments have four strings, though the range may be extended down by a "C-string attachment"—a device allowing the bass string to be lengthened and stopped mechanically.

© DIAGRAM

Harps

The modern harp is a regular member of the symphony orchestra. Its range is the largest of all orchestral instruments, and it is equally effective playing both solo melodies and the rippling chordal accompaniments with which it is most often associated. Interest in the harp as an orchestral instrument was developed in the 19th century by composers such as Wagner and Tchaikovsky, and still continues today.

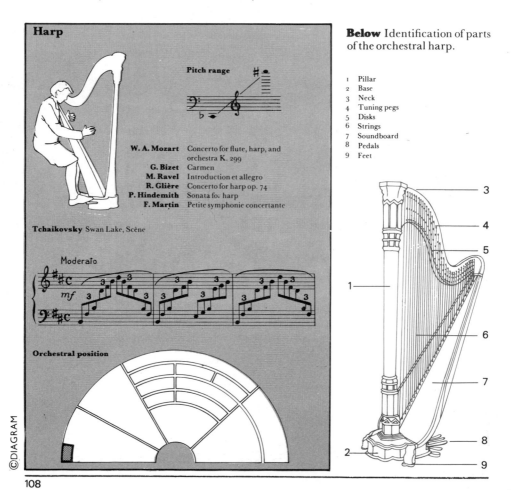

Harp

Pitch range

W. A. Mozart	Concerto for flute, harp, and orchestra K. 299
G. Bizet	Carmen
M. Ravel	Introduction et allegro
R. Glière	Concerto for harp op. 74
P. Hindemith	Sonata for harp
F. Martin	Petite symphonie concertante

Tchaikovsky Swan Lake, Scène

Moderato

mf

Orchestral position

Below Identification of parts of the orchestral harp.

1 Pillar
2 Base
3 Neck
4 Tuning pegs
5 Disks
6 Strings
7 Soundboard
8 Pedals
9 Feet

©DIAGRAM

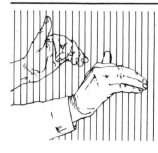 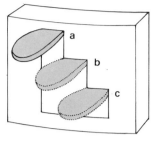 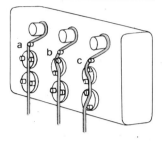

Above Diagram showing the playing position of the hands. The player may pluck strings singly or in chords. Some of the strings are colored to act as guides. Very attractive is the "glissando" effect obtained by running the hands across the strings, plucking each of them in quick succession.

Above Double-action pedal. With the pedal in position (a) the strings produce their natural note. Position (b) raises them a semitone, and (c) a full tone.

Above Diagram showing the operation of the disk mechanism that changes the pitch of the strings on the modern orchestral harp. In position (a) the disks have no effect on the string which therefore produces its natural note. In position (b) the studs of the top disk shorten the vibrating length of the string and raise its note by a semitone. In position (c) both disks are in contact with the string and raise its note by a full tone.

Right A modern concert harp—with double-action pedals. The double-action mechanism, invented in the 19th century, allows the player to raise the pitch of the strings by either a semitone or a tone. This has made it easier for the player to realize the instrument's full potential.

Elysian Concert Harp, J. George
Morley, London

Guitars

Today the guitar enjoys tremendous popularity in many parts of the world. The non-electric guitar is a light portable instrument that lends itself well to many forms of music. It is ideal for solos and for accompanying singing or other instruments. The classical or Spanish guitar has changed little since the 16th century, but popular folk guitars are now produced in a variety of different styles.

Right Classical or Spanish guitar. The six strings, traditionally gut, are now often nylon. The player demonstrates the classical playing position, with the guitar held centrally in front of his body. Plucking rather than strumming the strings is the essence of classical playing technique.

©DIAGRAM

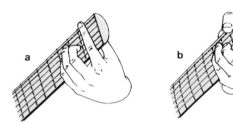

a   b

Left Fingering the sixth string. On the classical guitar (a) the player uses "barre" fingering, stopping the string with his index finger. The steel-strung guitar (b) has a narrower fingerboard with an oval cross-section, and the sixth string can be stopped from behind with the thumb.

1   2   3

Below Identification of parts of the modern classical guitar.

1   Machine head
2   Peg
3   Nut
4   Fingerboard
5   Frets
6   Sound hole
7   Body
8   Strings
9   Bridge

©DIAGRAM

Above Guitar heads. On the traditional guitar (1) the strings are tied to tuning pegs. On most modern guitars (2 and 3) the strings are threaded through machine heads, which fit into the head of the guitar. The string tension is changed by cogs when the tuning pegs are adjusted.

Below Bridges. On the classical guitar (a) the strings are threaded through holes in the bridge and tied. On the modern guitar (b) the strings end in rings that are inserted in holes in the bridge and secured with pins. On type (c) the strings thread through the tailpiece and the bridge is movable.

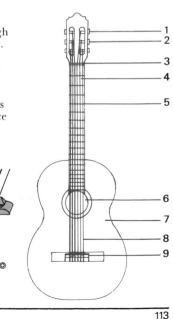

a   b   c

1
2
3
4
5
6
7
8
9

Modern grand pianos

The piano is one of the most popular and versatile of all instruments. It has a large pitch range, exceeded only by that of the organ, and is capable of great expressiveness. It remains important in the home where it is used both as a solo and accompanying instrument. The piano appears regularly on the concert platform in solo recitals and in performances of chamber music and concertos.

Below Modern grand piano. The grand's main advantages are that its open lid helps project the sound, and the floor beneath the soundboard reflects rather than absorbs sound. The center pedal, an optional extra, sustains only notes whose keys are depressed when the pedal is applied.

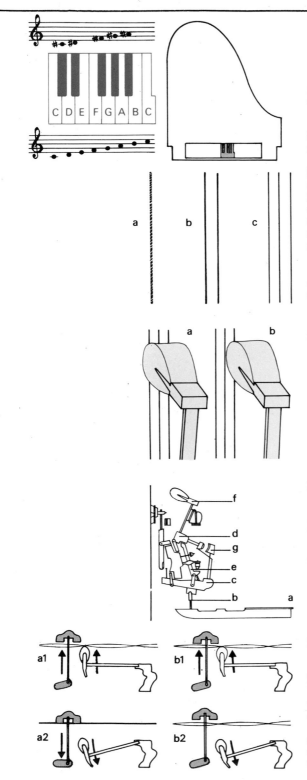

Left Notes comprising an octave on the piano. The keyboard is an excellent device for simplifying the playing of a complex stringed instrument. Keyboard instruments have existed for 700 years, and by the early 1400s the keys were arranged in the same order as on the modern piano.

Left Stringing on the modern piano. Each of the instrument's bass notes has only one string (a), whereas middle notes each have two finer strings (b), and top notes three still finer ones (c). All piano strings are made of steel, but bass strings are copper-wound to increase their resonance.

Left The action of the left, or "soft," pedal. When the pedal is not being used, the hammers strike the strings near their center (a). When the pedal is depressed, the hammers shift slightly to the right (b). This reduces contact with the strings and so produces a softer tone.

Left Upright action. When the key (a) is depressed, the pivot (b) lifts the lever (c) which then lifts the jack (d). This strikes the butt (e), throwing the hammer (f) against the string. The check (g) catches the hammer halfway on its return to make possible the more rapid repetition of notes.

Left Diagrams showing damper action. When a key is depressed, the dampers leave the strings (a1, b1). Usually they return to stop the strings vibrating as soon as the finger leaves the key (a2). Depressing the sustaining pedal delays damper action on all strings until the foot is raised (b2).

© DIAGRAM

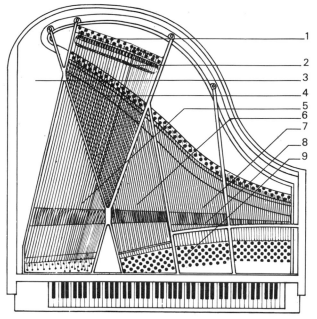

1 Hitch pins
2 Bass bridge
3 Soundboard
4 Long bridge
5 Single strings
6 Bichords
7 Trichords
8 Dampers
9 Wrest pins

Left Parts of a modern grand piano. The one-piece iron frame allows the strings to be stretched at high tension, improving the tone quality and responsiveness of the instrument. Small grands are cross-strung to accommodate the long bass strings in a shorter case.

Piano

Pitch range

W. A. Mozart — Piano quartet in B♭ major K.254
L. van Beethoven — "Emperor" concerto no. 5 in E♭ major op. 73
F. Chopin — Nocturnes, waltzes, polonaises
S. Rachmaninov — Piano concerto no. 2 in C minor
C. Debussy — La fille aux cheveux de lin

Brahms — Intermezzo op. 119

Andante teneramente

Position with orchestra

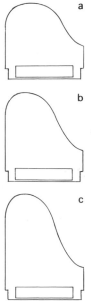

Above Diagram showing the three most important sizes of grand piano. The compact miniature or "baby" grand (a) is usually between 5ft 6in and 5ft 10in long. The drawing room or boudoir instrument (b) measures between 6ft and 7ft, and the concert grand (c) is 7ft to 9ft long.

© DIAGRAM

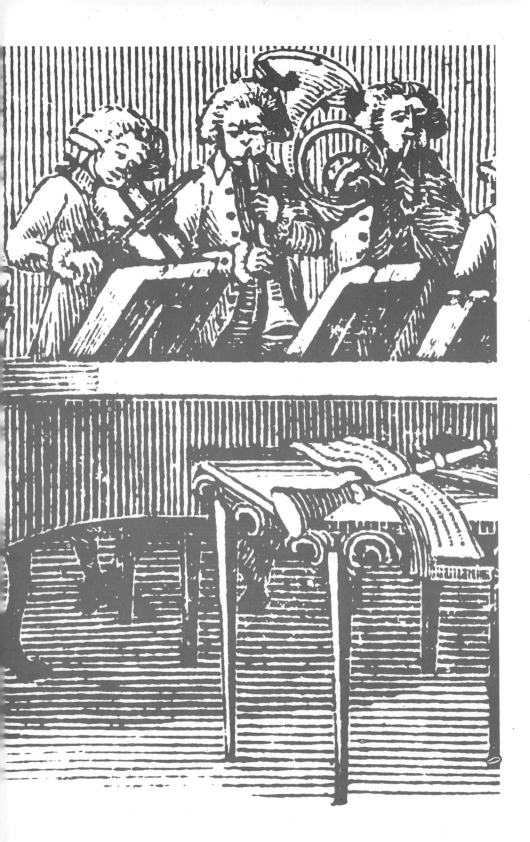

INDEX